THE

8 STRATEGIES TO NAVIGATING THE NEW NORMAL

PERVIN SHAIKH / ADRIAN SHEPHERD
JAMES WAHBA

COPYRIGHT © 2023 PERVIN SHAIKH / ADRIAN SHEPHERD / JAMES WAHBA

All rights reserved. No part of this book may be used or reproduced by any means, graphic, electronic, or mechanical, including photocopying, recording, taping, or by any information storage retrieval system, without the written permission of the publisher except in the case of brief quotations embodied in critical articles and reviews.

TABLE OF CONTENTS

CHAPTER 1: A ROUGH DAY 1
    Earlier That Morning 1
    At The Office 2
    The Aftermath 3
    The Coffee Shop 5
    The Long Trek Home 6
    Rooftop Gathering 7
    The First Small Step 8
    The Gym 9

CHAPTER 2: HEALTH 11
    Physiology Precedes Psychology 14
    Back At The Gym 15
    Yoga 17
    The Transformation Begins 18
    Sleep 20
    Christine 21

CHAPTER 3: DEALING WITH THE CAREER CURVEBALL 23
    Job Hunting Blues 23
    False Assurances 24
    The Consuming Job-Hunt 24

Marching On 25

Dream vs. Reality.. 25

One Step Ahead 26

Cost of Living.. 27

Reboot & Recharge 27

No Lucky Break 28

Rethinking The Job Hunt.. 28

Crickets 29

Serendipity.. 29

Anthony's World... 31

Shock Exit 32

Going Solo – The Hard Work 32

Leaving The Old World Behind 33

Words of Wisdom... 34

Self-Awareness Leads To Greater Clarity 35

The Chatter in the Head... 37

Post-Chatter Analysis 38

How Could She Take Back Control? 39

CHAPTER 4: CAREER TRANSFORMATION – THE REALITY . 40

At The Café 40

A Journey Of Self Discovery 41

Startup Woes.. 42

Trust Is Fragile 43

Lessons Learnt 44

Dealing With Difficult Conversations 44

Not Everyone Is Out There To Screw You 45

Trust Is Fragile 45

Expect The Unexpected 46

Ditch Other People's Judgements 47

Inner Circle Audit 47

Receiving A Blank Canvas Each Day 48

Setting Intentions 49

Ray of Hope 49

Career SWOT 50

CHAPTER 5: ADJUSTING TO THE NEW NORMAL 53

Journal Entry 54

Starting Over Again 56

The New Normal Routine 56

Plan to Succeed 57

Unlearn to Relearn 58

Journal Your Way To Success 60

Possibilities Are Endless With The Right Mindset 62

Feast and Famine Cycle 62

Shaking It Up A Bit 63

Find Your Champions 63

Keyboard Warrior Fatigue 64

CHAPTER 6: PRODUCTIVITY 65

Summary 66

The Productivity Pyramid 68

Personal Development 68

Habits 72

Strategies 74

Technology 76

Anthony's List of Books 79

CHAPTER 7: CREATING THE RIGHT ENVIRONMENT 80

Working From Home 81

Find The Best Method For You 83

Trial and Error 84

Making The Bed 85

Trying Different Places 85

Consistency Leads To Results 87

Sharing The Experiences 88

The Dreaded Buzz 89

Marie Kondo for Business 90

Journal Entry 91

CHAPTER 8: MASTERMIND 92

Your First Mastermind 94

Your New Support System 96

Oprah Winfrey & Co. 98

CHAPTER 9: TAKING CONTROL OF YOUR SCHEDULE 102
- When The Schedule Goes AWOL 102
- Taking Back Control 104
- Working From Home Loses Its Shine 105
- Build Your Support Group 106
- Clubhouse 107
- Working From Home Challenges 108
- Creating Boundaries 110

CHAPTER 10: A LEFT TURN 113
- Don't Take Your Foot Off the Accelerator 114
- Light at the End of the Tunnel 115
- Opportunities Aplenty 115
- Keep Learning 116
- Build Bridges 118
- The New World of Work 119
- The Coffee Shop Revisited 120
- One Last Piece of Advice 121
- A New Beginning 125

CHAPTER 1

A ROUGH DAY

"WTF am I going to do?"

Even Joanna was surprised to hear those words come out of her mouth.

It was 2:30 in the afternoon, and she was not at the office where she'd usually be but at her favorite coffee shop.

Her body language spoke volumes.

She was slouched over, looking at her phone in disbelief.

Her coffee was stone cold as she'd been sitting there for the past two hours trying to make sense of what had just happened.

She knew friends and heard stories about classmates struggling with work or money, but neither had ever been a problem for her.

At least, they hadn't been until today.

Earlier That Morning

It had been a bad year for so many.

Even Joanna's prestigious corporate Law firm had not been immune from the financial challenges presented by the pandemic.

As a result, the partners decided in Q2 2022 to start making contingency plans and aggressively looked at cutting costs in all business areas.

No department was immune from the changes.

She'd heard through the grapevine that a few key clients were in dire financial straits and unable to meet their financial obligations; it was highly likely they were insolvent.

That was bad news; Joanna knew it too and was well aware of the implications for her company.

Thankfully, her team would be ok.

After all, they were working on a high-profile deal which made her team pretty much indispensable, or so she thought.

As Joanna walked into the office from the Subway, she was surprised at where her thoughts led her.

Rumors had flown around like wildfire before, but Joanna wasn't worried. She asked, 'What would I do if my job was on the line?"

She quickly dismissed it because the reality didn't bear thinking about it.

Instead, she knew what she expected to do that day - A full day of client meetings and drafting a response.

At The Office

As she arrived, she noticed Patrick was in the office. He was never in before 10 am.

As a partner, he usually worked remotely on Monday mornings, so seeing him in the office was strange.

She wondered what was going on because he looked deep in thought.

Maybe it was to do with the deal they were working on, as the client had been pushing for financial year-end completion.

Patrick said he wanted to see her in his office as she settled down. She grabbed her laptop and headed to his office, coffee in hand.

As she entered, she knew something was up because Patrick wasn't his usual talkative self. Instead, he seemed stiff and uncomfortable.

When she saw Tara, she knew it was serious.

She frantically started thinking about what could have gone wrong for HR to be present.

He started talking about the reorganization and how the management team was looking to streamline services.

Suddenly, the other shoe dropped.

"I'm so sorry, Joanna, but we're going to have to let you go." She didn't catch the rest.

Suddenly she felt like she was having an out-of-body experience and thought this wasn't happening to her but to someone else.

The Aftermath

Joanna was caught by surprise.

After 15 minutes, Patrick suggested she go out and get some fresh air and come back again later in the week to discuss the details with HR.

Patrick was trying to be empathetic and assured Joanna that he would be there if she needed to talk.

However, he did ask that she would not say anything to the others until the paperwork was complete.

All Joanna could think of was who would do her share of the work, especially as more work would be done on the deal.

Patrick assured her all her work would be assigned to her colleagues and that she not worry. A handover meeting would also occur tomorrow, and Joanna could dial in remotely.

He had also scheduled an appointment with HR later that week to work through the paperwork, and Joanna would have a chance to review the documents thoroughly.

Joanna felt stunned as the news started to sink in.

Suddenly, she felt exhausted, and weeks and months of working long hours seemed to catch up. Joanna just wanted to get out of the building.

But she didn't know where to go once she was out.

Maybe she should go to Blue Bottle Coffee and take stock of what had happened, or she should go home. What she wanted was to get more details.

Did she get fired? Were other people going to be laid off too?

What about severance pay?

She snapped out of it just long enough to realize that she was standing in front of Blue Bottle.

The Coffee Shop

$32,634.95.

Joanna could hardly believe it, but that was the number staring back at her on her iPhone.

At present, it was all the money in the world she had.

Well, that and her last paycheck plus severance, which she'd receive in a few weeks.

Just how much severance, she'd have to wait and see.

Not bad considering everything that had happened, but the rent of her one-bedroom apartment in Williamsburg, Brooklyn, was not cheap.

At $4500 a month, along with her student loan, and other expenses, Joanna calculated she had a little over six months to figure out what she would do next.

This was uncharted territory for her.

Where had she gone wrong?

Joanna had always been smart, graduating cum laude from Columbia University and landing herself a dream career.

She was a hard worker, and people seemed to like her. Her clients were happy.

She got along with her coworkers, and her boss' reviews were always glowing.

As a result, her salary has steadily risen over the past few years. Something she was quite proud of.

She had always been good with money, putting aside 10% of her salary for years.

Unfortunately, her big mistake was trusting the wrong financial planner.

She couldn't believe her luck. Last week, she had gotten a call from him regarding her stocks and learned that her funds had been frozen due to the fund's financial irregularities.

There was no way of knowing how much and, more importantly, when she'd have access to them.

It's one thing to have $124,000 in your funds and another when you can't access them, as Joanna would soon learn.

The one thing she could always fall back on was her job.

But now, that has gone up in smoke.

The Long Trek Home

Now what? Why couldn't she think straight?

Joanna mustered up enough energy to climb the stairs, having caught the wrong train.

Each step began to feel like a lead; all she wanted to do was get home.

Maybe she should call someone, but who?

Everyone was working, and her folks were the last people she wanted to reach.

Besides, they had their challenges to worry about.

Three days went by in one big blur. A text on her phone snapped her out of it.

It was Sam, and she had texted to remind her of the rooftop social invite in the building.

She still hadn't told anyone apart from Sam, who was trying to be sympathetic.

Still, it was the last thing she needed, and she didn't feel like going tonight, especially because she would be surrounded by people getting on with their careers and lives.

Rooftop Gathering

Social Sam had arrived on the dot and insisted she put on a nice top, paint her face, and get ready to go, as it would do her a world of good.

"Joanna, how long can you stay cooped up in the apartment? It's not the end of the world."

If it weren't for Sam, Joanna would have canceled.

"You're smart, and you'll find something very soon. Just come for a little while and have a couple of drinks."

Brendan, who had known her for years, found her particularly quiet and asked her how she was doing and how the project was going because he knew what a big deal it was.

She decided to come clean and told him and the others what had happened.

Amidst the sympathetic hugs and assurances, she felt very alone.

Inevitably, the same questions swirling around her mind were suddenly being asked out loud.

What happened?

How do you feel?

What was she going to do now?

Was she looking for a change of scenery?

Her resume wasn't up-to-date, and she'd been out of the job-hunting game for so long.

She tried not to think about it and answered everyone's questions to the best of her ability.

The truth was, though, she didn't know.

The employees in the group were the most challenging to deal with because it was so hard to alleviate their concerns.

The entrepreneurs, on the other hand, were very upbeat and gave her some encouragement.

"Time to set up your practice," said Chris.

Matt chimed in with his usual bravado, "I remember when that happened to me years ago.

The best thing that ever happened to me."

Cynthia also said what nobody had done all day, saying, "Honey, welcome to my world. Now we can be ladies who have lunch."

But, of course, that's the last thing Joanna wanted to be - a lady who lunched.

It was a rough night. She felt alone and discouraged.

It was the first time since she had sat at the Bar that she felt this anxious.

The First Small Step

While Joanna had let herself wallow in self-pity the past few days, the rooftop get-together had at least brought things to the surface.

The following morning, instead of spending the morning in bed as she had been, she woke up at 8 am and started getting her thoughts out on paper.

As she did, she remembered something someone said in an interview she'd read a while back.

What exactly, she was hazy on. It had something to do with exercise. Essentially movement changes how you feel.

She figured, what did she have to lose? So, she decided to head to the gym the next day.

After all, she had been paying her gym membership for years but never really gotten much use out of it. Now seemed like the perfect time to do so.

The Gym

She left early Wednesday morning, determined to go to the SoulCycle class first and work through the anger and frustrations that had been building up since she'd gotten the news.

She was particularly annoyed about how the company made the handover call the day after letting her go so briefly and transactionally.

But they were moving forward, and her colleague Jonathan would take over all the work she'd put in, and that was it.

"Is this how corporations operate?" She thought to herself.

The team's sentiments touched her after they heard because it was a shocking announcement. Nevertheless, it didn't make it any less painful.

However, she knew they'd be busy with their weekly deadlines, and Joanna would quickly become an afterthought.

Having spoken to HR during the week, she found out more details about the severance package.

As approved by Patrick, she had three months' severance pay and a discretionary payment of $1000.

She wanted to feel in control again and didn't want other people to pity or give her sympathy.

After SoulCycle class, she felt more energetic and decided to work on her resume because she was determined to send it out on Monday at the latest to a list of law firms and friends in the industry.

CHAPTER 2

HEALTH

It blows anyone's ego when things go from good to bad overnight.

For Joanna, it was especially tough as she'd never really struggled before. She always knew what to do.

Not now.

She didn't realize how much her being let go had affected her, but the signs were there. Had any of her friends popped over, they would have known something was off.

Dishes sat in the sink till after lunch, her bed unmade, her hair disheveled.

That's not who Joanna was. But things like this can have a weird effect on people.

They may seem insignificant, but for someone who had it all together, they were the telltale signs of depression, albeit small.

Despite venturing out a few weeks ago to her SoulCycle class, she hadn't been since.

She had sent out her resume and a bunch of emails, but all she'd gotten back was crickets. That wasn't something Joanna had expected.

As a result, she regressed.

Now she was spending much of her time at home surfing the web, watching Netflix and discovering new ice cream flavors.

Her favorite so far has been Talenti Peppermint Bark Gelato.

There's no telling how long she would have stayed in her funk if not for Tim's call.

Despite being adversaries from time to time when he worked for Bank Of America, they would get together from time to time to exchange war stories.

Tim was one of her closest colleagues when he joined the firm.

However, he moved to another firm a few years back when they gave him an offer he couldn't refuse.

Joanna was surprised to see his name on her phone and was tempted to let it go to voicemail, but for whatever reason, she just wanted someone to listen to her, and Tim was as good as anyone.

Tim was surprised to hear that she'd been laid off but understood that times were tough in the industry. He listened to Joanna ramble on for a good 30 minutes or so.

He had always been a good listener.

It would have probably ended there were it not for Tim asking her one question.

"When was the last time you got a haircut?"

Of everything Tim could have said, Joanna certainly didn't expect that.

"I ask because a friend of mine got canned a few years back and she sort of fell apart.

She started gaining weight and didn't seem to care about her appearance including her hair.

She stopped doing much of anything and really let herself go. When she finally got to the salon, she came back with a slick new hairdo and a whole new attitude.

It really kickstarted jolt-started her recovery". Joanna had to think about when she got a haircut.

She had no idea what day it was, much less the last time she'd gotten a haircut.

Without checking her calendar, she couldn't answer him. That hit her like a sledgehammer.

Joanna was so quiet Tim thought the line had disconnected.

It was at that moment Joanna realized something needed to change.

Or, more appropriately, SHE needed to change.

She got up and looked around her apartment.

Her bed, the dishes, and even her mirror reflection told a story that she didn't like.

She told Tim she'd call him back as she had something to do.

What exactly? Joanna didn't know, but something…anything.

She washed the dishes and put them away in the cupboards; she made her bed, tidied up her coffee table, and then started putting her closet in order.

"It's not much," Joanna said to herself when she finished, "but it's a start."

Joanna thought about her next move.

Nothing came to mind, but then she remembered where she'd read that article about the importance of exercise.

It had been in one of her Entrepreneur magazines.

She dug through the pile of magazines she'd kept at the back of her closet. She pulled them out and started going through them.

It didn't take her long.

"Aha, there it is," she said to herself.

Physiology Precedes Psychology

It was an article on Tony Robbins, the so-called personal development guru.

She never really put much faith in that stuff as she found it a bit wishy-washy, but for whatever reason, that article had left an impression.

Joanna remembered it was focused on life change.

She flipped through the pages and found the article.

At the top of the page was a quote from Robbins in caps "MOTION CREATES EMOTION."

She sat down on the floor there and read through the article quickly.

It talked about the six basic needs of people, the mistakes people make, the excuses people have, and for Joanna, most importantly, how to change your mental state.

In a nutshell, Robbins explained the fastest way to affect change in your life was through changing your physiology.

"Motion, huh?" thought Joanna.

Her SoulCycle class had been good.

Joanna had to admit, though, she hadn't felt much like going out since then.

"Well, while I'm waiting for responses, I might as well give it a shot," she said to herself as if she were talking to Robbins.

She grabbed her phone, logged into her gym app, and booked a session for the following day.

This time, however, she decided that she might as well book the next five days straight for the early class.

That way, it would get her out of bed.

Back At The Gym

The following day, Joanna woke up at 7:25, after the third snooze alarm went off.

She made herself some breakfast which, unlike recently, was hot.

She got to the gym at 8:15 sharp, changed, and then did an hour of SoulCycle.

She was planning to head home after that, but she happened to see a yoga lesson in progress.

Rather than leave, she decided to pop in and give it a go.

Thankfully there weren't that many people in the class, so she borrowed a yoga mat and placed it towards the back of the room.

She hadn't done yoga in years, and it showed. Her flexibility was nothing like it used to be, which surprised her. She'd always been flexible when she was young.

That evening her body was so sore she decided to do something she never did – take a bath.

She remembered watching a documentary on Japan and how people there took a bath every night.

Despite Hollywood glamorizing baths in movies like Pretty Woman, people in the West hardly use their bathtubs.

Instead, they opt for a quick shower to wake themselves up in the morning.

"Not tonight," she thought. "I'm gonna get my Julia Roberts on."

Soaking her tired body in the bath was just what she needed. While it wasn't easy, Joanna had to admit it felt good.

By the end of the week, she had even made a few new friends at the gym, one of whom, Christine, asked her if she would like to grab a coffee sometime.

Joanna said sure, so they planned to go out next week when Christine's kids were back in school.

Christine was a few years older than Joanna, chattier and more outgoing but grounded, so they got along well.

Over coffee, Christine talked about her kids, her husband, work, life in general, and Joanna's newfound interest in the gym.

"You just joined, didn't you?" Christine asked.

Joanna explained how she had been a member for years but had barely had the time to come.

"I remember those days well," Christine said. "I used to think I was 'too busy.'

Then I realized that it was all just an excuse. We're always busy.

We either make time for it, or we don't. Finally, I just said, 'Screw it.' Been here ever since."

Joanna chuckled. She supposed that had something to do with having three kids.

Christine wasn't one to beat around the bush.

Christine told her how she had started with yoga, then joined SoulCycle and added some weight training to help shed some of those extra pounds she had put on during pregnancy.

Joanna had never been fat, but she certainly hadn't taken good care of her body the last few years.

Poor sleeping habits, logging long hours to get ahead and very little, if any, exercise. The combination had taken its toll.

Christine was right, though. She could have made time to get to the gym; it hadn't been a priority for her.

The more Christine talked, the more inspired Joanna became.

Yoga

Joanna had never done weight training before but figured she'd give it a shot the next day.

She made sure to charge her Apple Airpods that night and update her music selection on iTunes. Beyonce, Taylor Swift, Eminem, and Ed Sheeran were a few that cut.

The thought of lifting weights didn't appeal to Joanna much, so she figured her jams would at least make it somewhat bearable.

It was rough.

Joanna had always prided herself in caring for herself, or at least she thought she did.

It was evident just how much she'd been sacrificing for her work.

She was out of shape, and it was apparent. Her strength was nowhere near what it was in college, and she was drenched in sweat in no time.

Every rep, every pull, every breath made her muscles burn.

She crawled to the shower after only 20 minutes.

Her body's aches and pains were a reminder of how little she'd taken care of her health working 14-hour shifts.

It was a wake-up call.

The Transformation Begins

Joanna hadn't sweated like this, well, ever.

Back in school, she was part of the volleyball team, but as Joanna was learning, exercise as an adult was completely different.

Parts of her body hurt that she didn't even know she had. She ached all over, but it was a good sort of ache.

A few weeks later, though, her body no longer ached.

She could join her SoulCycle class and spend 45 minutes in the weight room.

The added workout had started affecting her diet.

Her cravings for chocolate and coffee were gone, replaced by her body's yearning for meat and water.

She had also cooked a lot more than eating out, but that had more to do with her bank account than her stomach.

She had never really cooked much before, but one night she'd come across some clips of Gordon Ramsey's Junior Masterchef on YouTube.

Seeing kids aged eight to 12 create what looked like Joanna as Michelin Star dishes inspired her to improve her cooking.

If they could do it, what excuse did she have?

Naturally, there was a slight learning curve, but being in control of her diet radically changed her energy levels.

She'd shrunk her portions and added more veggies to her meals.

Joanna's mother had been the typical housewife back in the day.

She prepared meals each night for the family.

Like most people, Joanna loved her mother's food, everything except vegetables.

Her mother mainly just threw them in a pot of boiling water, and that was that.

As a result, Joanna saw vegetables as a mere necessity.

YouTube had opened her eyes to just how great vegetables could be.

Her stomach, as well as her muscles, thanked her.

Shopping for ingredients was one of the things she now looked forward to.

Something she thought she'd never do.

She thought back to her corporate days and realized that friends, colleagues or clients were constantly asking out the main reason she hardly cooked.

That's big city life, she thought.

For those nights when she was free, there was also the ease of just picking something up at a restaurant on her way home or when she was too tired, she didn't mind paying the extra for UberEats.

"Desperate times call for desperate measures," she had told herself, looking at her back account balance dropping.

As it turned out, though, it was a blessing in disguise. She felt healthier than she had in years.

Sleep

It wasn't just the exercise and the new diet that was responsible for her feeling so much better.

Her new workout was kicking her butt.

The moment her head hit the pillow each night, she was out.

Her body was exhausted.

It didn't hurt that she was caffeine-free for the first time since college.

What was interesting, though, was that despite being so tired at each day's end, she woke up slightly earlier than before and felt much more alive.

Joanna did some sleuthing and was surprised to find out that the more exercise you get, the less sleep you need.

It sounded somewhat counterintuitive, but she wasn't complaining.

Christine

"It'll take a while," Christine said. She caught Joanna looking at herself in the mirror.

"What? Oh, yeah, I know." But Joanna couldn't help but think about what she used to look like.

She used to have a great body, but the lack of exercise and abuse she endured over the years left her looking like someone ten years older.

Joanna was a woman who didn't buy into the fat acceptance movement.

She hadn't noticed how her lifestyle had been affecting her.

"If you're fat, then do something about it" was her belief.

"Staying fit gets harder as you get older. But that doesn't mean it can't be done.

After my third kid, it took me a whole year to regain my figure. If I can do it, you can, too."

Christine had become a good friend.

She helped Joanna develop her workout routine and advised her what to avoid.

It was great to talk to someone who didn't know her

She could open up to her about everything she was going through.

She had kept most of her friends in the dark about what she was going through.

Christine could relate. It had been hard for her, many of her friends were still living a single life after she had kids.

"I'm grateful I've got you to talk to. I haven't told most of my friends what happened." Joanna said as they were changing.

"Friends are great, but sometimes they don't tell us what we need to hear," Christine responded.

Joanna nodded in agreement.

"It's just hard when they can't relate."

Christine explained how her new lifestyle of being a parent and gym rat had lost some friends.

They couldn't understand why she wanted to get in shape.

"Losing friends? Over getting in shape?"

The thought had never occurred to Joanna, but she had to admit that going to the gym meant less time doing other activities, aka time with friends.

"I guess you just have to make a choice."

"Exactly," Christine replied. "I chose to get in shape for my family and me.

It's not easy raising three kids when your husband travels.

Swim practices, ballet recitals, and taking care of the house on top of work are tough.

Finding time to squeeze in the gym was tough.

But I did it."

Joanna had nothing but respect for this woman standing in front of her.

A mother and an employee still managed to find time to stay in shape.

CHAPTER 3

DEALING WITH THE CAREER CURVEBALL

Physically Joanna was doing better, but career-wise it was another matter.

Joanna felt like she was going around in circles.

Her job-hunt strategy worked very well for her the last time, so she didn't understand what was going wrong this time.

She knew deep down she didn't want any of the roles in the market, but that was all she knew.

Plus it would buy her some time whilst she tried to 'figure it out.'

Job Hunting Blues

Every time she sat down to do some job-hunting, she felt a sense of dread.

The feeling stayed with her for the best part of the day.

Her head and her heart were saying something completely different.

Joanna noticed she had a tendency for her head to override what her heart was feeling.

If she listened to her heart, it would require too much introspection, and right now, she didn't fancy opening up a can of worms.

Joanna was usually a rational thinker, and 99% of the time, her mind would rule over her heart.

False Assurances

So to help her get through it, she prepared herself mentally and consoled herself by saying it would only be for a short while.

She was usually ok in the mornings because that's when she worked at her best.

She'd learnt to tackle the most difficult tasks head-on to feel in control at work.

She couldn't even remember the last time she went out and had a carefree evening with her friends.

However, it was usually after lunch when her motivational levels would start to drop, and her mind would wander.

By the end of the day, she felt spent.

The Consuming Job-Hunt

Going out felt like a luxury, a world away from the one she was used to. Instead, the job hunt was eating up all of her free time.

When she did sit down, each application was beginning to feel like an uphill struggle.

Each question sounded the same but with different words.

She knew she was going through the job-hunt motions and ending up "copying and pasting" answers from other applications.

She felt her applications were lackluster, and she knew this would come across to a potential employer.

It was hardly surprising that she received rejection after rejection, sometimes several times a day.

It was also beginning to have an impact on her confidence.

Marching On

Nevertheless, Joanna battled on.

The job hunt was exhausting, but Joanna had enough mental grit to scout the job boards and LinkedIn job section each day – just in case she missed something.

She set up alerts on LinkedIn and received multiple notifications for roles.

For some, she was overqualified; for others, she was under qualified, or the job was on the other side of the country.

Sometimes, she got lost in other job descriptions in non-corporate roles. She realized there was a big world out there.

But, the more she looked at them, the inner voice of discontent just got louder.

Job hunting was never a breeze at the best of times.

She knew this from her experience but back then, the market was different, and she knew her stellar resume had opened some new doors.

However, this time around, it was another ball game.

Dream vs. Reality

Like many of her contemporaries, Joanna thought they would sail through the career ladder.

However, the motto amongst her peers was "Work hard, play hard and kick-ass".

They'd sacrificed so much by attending good schools and getting good grades. Therefore they felt they had paid their dues.

Joanna had been good at building relationships with her bosses and other seniors familiar with her work ethic.

She was usually one of the first to come into the office and among the last to leave on many occasions.

She was also known for taking work home with her.

One Step Ahead

She did this to stay above the rest of her peers, especially regarding promotions.

She knew to get to Director and Partner level, she would have to be exceptional.

It was a given. Work hard and climb high.

But now, she sat back and thought.

Maybe this career setback was a blessing in disguise, but she wasn't in the mood to be reflective.

Instead, she just wanted to be economically active again.

She'd always wanted to try another career but didn't pursue it while working frantic long hours and most weekends.

She didn't have time to breathe, let alone think about anything else.

Cost of Living

Finances dictated the shots, and even with all the cuts she made, living in NY was not cheap.

She would need to get something quickly.

However, time was not on her side, and if she didn't secure something soon, her bank account would start to feel the pinch.

It was getting something quickly, which was the biggest challenge.

She could not be fussy because there weren't many suitable roles.

There didn't seem to be many roles out there, either.

She would have to take the next opportunity that came along.

Reboot & Recharge

She took a hiatus from job-hunting for a couple of days to collect her thoughts and motivate herself.

When she returned, she was determined to reboot her job hunt and return to the drawing board with a revised action plan.

She always felt this way every time she looked at her bank balance.

But then, suddenly, she felt an extra push to get on with the job hunt.

All she needed was a lucky break somewhere.

However, it didn't take long before she felt a gnawing feeling in her stomach.

It was a reasonably straightforward recruitment process, albeit a series of gruelling interviews.

She knew she would deliver an excellent performance once she got in front of an interviewer.

No Lucky Break

But that was proving to be the biggest challenge. It worked for her the last time.

She had wowed the law firm, and they couldn't wait to hire her.

So why couldn't she replicate the same process now?

Maybe she was doing the job hunting wrong.

Rethinking The Job Hunt

The last time she was job hunting, she worked from morning until night and could easily knock out applications one after the other.

She knew she was using the "Spray and Pray approach" by sending her resume to every hiring company she could think of.

It made her feel like she was doing something useful, but it was counterproductive.

Previously, her networking strategy worked as well.

She sent emails to friends and their network.

That's how she landed the role at the law firm.

She knew Patrick's friend Brianna who mentioned that the law firm was looking for bright young professionals.

However, during the pandemic, the network had dried up as many other law firms were cutting headcount too.

Many responded politely, saying they would look out for something and let her know.

Crickets

But rarely did she hear back. Joanna knew it wasn't their fault; it was a sign of the times.

Each day she felt she was being busy for the sake of being active, and at the end of the day, she felt resigned to the unrelenting job hunt grind.

She read on one of the job boards that job hunting during the pandemic was like a full-time job.

Boy, did she know that feeling?

Joanna knew she still lacked focus and did what she did before – send as many applications out and pray someone would notice her skills and experience.

What she failed to acknowledge was the fact that the business world had changed since her college days.

As a result, Joanna was feeling increasingly frustrated.

Serendipity

Joanna went to the coffee shop for a couple of hours to finish yet another job application.

As she added the final touches, she got a text message from Christine telling her that she wouldn't be able to come to the gym for a while due to family matters.

"Family matters could be anything," Joanna thought.

She wrote the obligatory if-you-need-anything message, but Christine said she didn't need anything and would get in touch with her once everything was sorted.

"What a shame," Joanna thought. She was getting used to having a gym buddy she could talk to.

As luck would have it, just then, out of the corner of her eye, she happened to see a familiar face, but she couldn't remember his name.

It was at the tip of her tongue. Maybe it's Tony. All of a sudden she remembered, it was "Anthony".

Anthony was ordering coffee, but he hadn't seen her.

She had seen Anthony around the gym and talked to him once briefly.

Normally she would have let him go about his business, but for some reason, she decided to get his attention.

She called his name, but he didn't hear her because the music played.

She called him again, and he turned around. 'Oh hey. It's Joanna, right?

How are you?' Anthony replied.

"Yes, you remembered," smiled Joanna. "I'm good, thanks," she replied.

She didn't want to talk about her current situation.

Instead, Joanna told Anthony she was job-hunting and using the coffee shop to work on her application.

'I hear the job hunt is a little challenging right now. How are you finding it?" asked Anthony.

"It's a lot tougher than I thought. Plus, it's time-consuming," replied Joanna.

"I can imagine. May I offer you some tips from my own experience? Said Anthony.

"Yeah, sure. Anything to help me get a job," responded Joanna.

Before Anthony proceeded, he told Joanna his story.

Anthony's World

Anthony had previously worked in the corporate world as a Banker for Gothman Soanes, a Tier 1 Investment Bank.

He felt lucky to get in, but the grind was real.

The hours were very long, and he had a demanding boss from day one.

There were no shortcuts to the top, and his boss ensured everyone in his team knew this right from the start.

Anthony committed wholeheartedly to the role.

He worked, on average, 90-100 hours in the first three years as an analyst.

He was promoted to Associate and then Vice President after two years.

He handled the pressure well, but it came at the expense of his personal life - he had none.

He told Joanna the reason for staying was because he wanted the Senior VP promotion.

However, it never came.

Shock Exit

Anthony knew the financial markets were volatile, but not being promoted to Senior VP was the last straw.

Upon reflection, he knew a promotion was not forthcoming because his boss would have indicated something.

He knew it was time to move on. It wasn't a matter of if but when.

That's precisely what he did.

A month later, he handed in his resignation letter, and that was that.

No job lined up. No safety net. Nothing. But Anthony felt it was the right move.

'Wow. Gutsy," thought Joanna.

Going Solo – The Hard Work

His family was shocked as they thought he loved the job and always talked about the travel and hard work he consistently did for clients.

However, they didn't realize how unhappy he had been.

In many ways, Joanna was like Anthony.

She never revealed the absolute truth about her career when she spoke to her family.

But, like Anthony's parents, Joanna's folks were none the wiser.

She wondered how many parents were oblivious to their offspring's predicaments at that moment.

She suspected not many!

Anthony's parents were even more concerned when he said he wanted to become an entrepreneur.

His friends' circle was also surprised, but they were supportive.

Two of his friends, who worked in Venture Capital, knew Anthony was ready for a significant change.

By this stage of their careers, they, too, wanted something different.

Anthony told Joanna it took a while for him to adjust.

It took even longer for his family and friends to understand his thinking.

A couple of his friends never did.

Leaving The Old World Behind

Anthony wasn't looking for a new job because he knew it would be more or less the same if he went elsewhere.

He was done with toxic bosses, backstabbing, office politics and the constant alpha jostling up the greasy career pole.

He felt confident now was the time to kick start some of his goals and dreams. However, in the beginning, he felt as if he were swimming upstream.

He thought that he had enough expertise and a big corporate name behind him that would help him, or so he thought.

"Wow," thought Joanna. Anthony had experienced his fair share of change during his career.

Words of Wisdom

The more she thought about the recent redundancy, the angrier she felt. Why did she even bother working such long hours?

Joanna had inadvertently tied her identity with her work.

As a result, she was experiencing low self-esteem.

Anthony sensed something was up and suggested a couple of simple exercises. One of them was called "Walk Through The Uncertainty."

Exercise 1 – Walk Through The Uncertainty

Anthony told her to put her sneakers on and walk it through. He told her:

✓ Don't think of anything, walk.

✓ If she didn't like walking, he suggested drawing, writing, dancing, reading or doing whatever helped her break the old thinking pattern.

✓ How long should the walk be? Start with 25 minutes and steadily build up to an hour.

✓ How often? Whatever works best.

What was so good about this exercise?

∗ ☐ It helped break old thinking pattern

∗ ☐ It gave a different perspective

∗ ☐ It enabled you to feel in control

* Over time, it would help develop better ideas and create fluid opportunities.

She decided to go for a long walk. Williamsburg had some great spots for walking, and it would do her a world of good to get outdoors.

After her first walk, Joanna wasn't any clearer after her first walk than when she first started, but it made her feel fresher.

It stopped the constant chatter in her head that was getting increasingly louder, and she noticed it had been getting increasingly hostile.

It was so not like her to think so pessimistically.

After the walk, she decided to pack her kit and hit the gym.

But then, she remembered what Anthony had said to her as they parted.

He suggested she monitor her Self-Talk or "internal chatter", as he called it, because this was likely to impact everything she did from when she woke up to when she went to sleep.

Self-Awareness Leads To Greater Clarity

Anthony was a massive fan of self-awareness, and self-talk was his favorite topic.

As Sam would put it, Anthony's 'rescue remedy.'

Anthony would fly around the world to different retreats and come back full of different techniques and ideas.

Anthony was also a voracious reader, and his room was filled with books on various subjects and authors the others hadn't even heard of.

Brenden was an old friend. Joanna was baffled by what Brendan had said.

How did this 'chatter' or self-talk affect her daily routine?

Joanna had a little bit of time before her next Yoga class.

It's a different world out there. So she quickly Googled "self-talk" on the internet.

There was so much information on it she didn't know where to start.

However, she found one article that was like a dummy's guide to self-talk.

'Phew'. She wasn't interested in the science behind self-talk; she just wanted to know what it was.

She read about the impact of words, tone and power on an individual.

It could make the difference between having a blah day or a blah experience and a fantastic one.

She made a note in the diary the moment she finished reading.

She wrote the following:

Self-Talk is the voice we hear when we wake up to sleep. The 'internal chatter' would play continuously and cannot be switched off.

However, what we can do is control the volume of our thoughts and the impact on our actions and behaviors

She also noted an exercise suggested on the sites.

It looked reasonably straightforward and something she could do immediately instead of waiting for the perfect moment.

The exercise was called "Chatter in the Head."

The Chatter in the Head

It suggested analyzing our present self-talk and looking out for the following:

✳ ☐ Look at chatter without judgment.

✳ ☐ Ditch the 'I should think like ...', or 'I could' or 'I would' narrative because it defeats the objective, plus it was like beating yourself up.

✳ ☐ Ask yourself if the chatter is Good/Bad/Helpful, or unhelpful.

✳ ☐ Look at the tone of the chatter – is it positive/negative or neutral?

✳ ☐ How does the chatter impact you?

✳ ☐ Learn to tune in, so you know when to tune out.

✳ ☐ Controlling the volume comes with experience, as you can't switch the chatter off.

She thought there was no time like the present; she decided to practice the self-talk exercise on the way to the gym.

Hopefully, this would help her feel better than she did before the walk. If the exercise didn't work, at least the gym would uplift her spirits.

Even before she got to the gym, she noticed something. Her self-talk was overwhelmingly negative.

She also noted that she was using the deadly trio, which were "should, could and would."

She also realized they were on autopilot and auto-loop.

It was constant, and the only time it seemed to die down was when she was distracted by activity or talking to someone else.

Post-Chatter Analysis

She noticed sentences/statements like:

'I should have saved more money.'

'I could move in with mum until I sort myself out.'

'I could have put more effort into my career development instead of leaving it for another time. Then maybe I wouldn't feel like I do now.'

'I'm trying too hard with the job hunt, but I'm not feeling the vibe.'

'Law is not really for me. So why do I still waste my time chasing something which won't make me happy again?'

'Maybe I'm not good enough anymore. If I were, I would get a role quickly.'

Joanna realized her negative self-talk was preventing her from moving forward.

It was impacting her confidence as well as her job hunt strategy. She went back three steps every time she tried to take action.

With each auxiliary verb, she was sabotaging her success, and instead of aiming high, she was aiming low.

She even surprised herself by applying to companies she wouldn't consider previously.

Joanna understood how self-talk impacted her, especially during different times of the day.

For example, she would feel upbeat in the morning and get a lot of work done. However, she was doing the bulk of the job hunt in the afternoon, when she was susceptible to doubts and mindset shifts.

How Could She Take Back Control?

Firstly, she would learn how to use her self-talk to her advantage.

How? Starting tomorrow, Joanna will monitor her self-talk and look out for times during the day when it impacts her the most.

She was keen to understand when and how her self-talk went against her.

Joanna came across a positive Self-Talk graphic online and downloaded it for future reference.

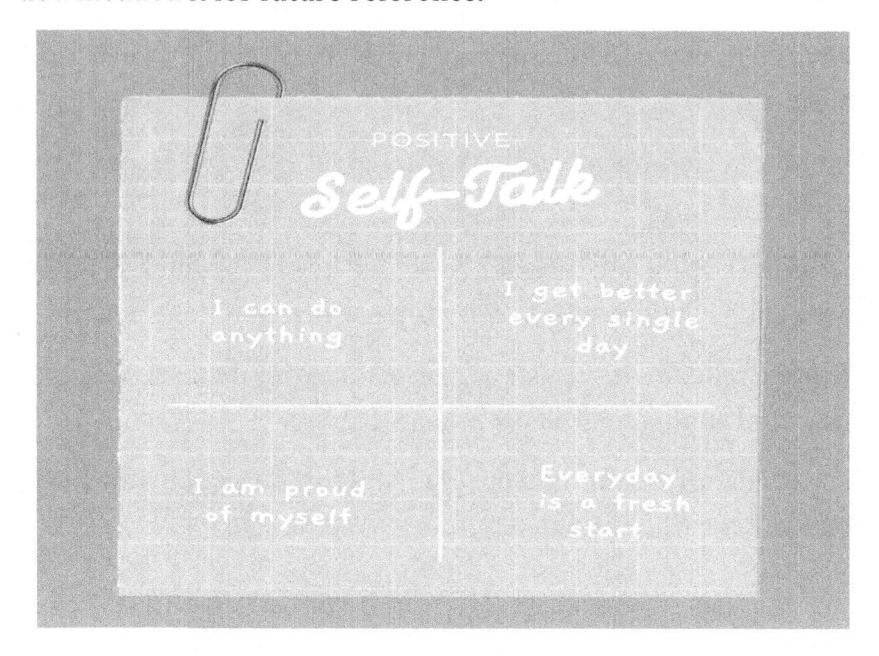

POSITIVE
Self-Talk

I can do anything

I get better every single day

I am proud of myself

Everyday is a fresh start

CHAPTER 4

CAREER TRANSFORMATION – THE REALITY

She was so absorbed in her train of thought she nearly missed Anthony in the gym reception. She hadn't seen him since they met in the coffee shop three weeks ago.

Anthony was always upbeat and ready to 'kick ass' each day, which was the opposite of Joanna's feelings.

"Hey Joanna, it's great to see you again. How's the job hunting going?

She told him the truth about her situation, and he said, "Look, Joanna, there's a lot of uncertainty out there.

Companies are cutting their workforce in significant numbers. You're not the only one going through a tough time.

"G. Michael Hopf famously said, 'Hard times create strong men, strong men create good times, good times create weak men, and weak men create hard times.' The question is which one you will be."

At The Café

He suggested they grab a coffee in the gym café after her session, and he would see if there might be a way for him to help her.

Once Joanna had finished her session in the gym, she felt much better and was ready to meet Anthony and absorb some of his pumped-up vibes.

She met Anthony in the café, and as he approached him, he said, "Nice to see you smiling, Joanna". Then, over a skinny oat milk extra frothy latte, he listened carefully to what Joanna had to say.

Anthony felt Joanna's frustrations, pain, and disappointment; at that moment, he was about to say something but then thought better of it.

He knew what she was going through. But kept quiet because Joanna had to experience the steps herself.

After she finished, he told her more about his start-up story, which he didn't talk about the last time they met.

He told her what he did to get back on his feet after experiencing his first significant entrepreneurial setback.

A Journey Of Self Discovery

When Anthony decided to leave Gothman Soanes, he embarked on a journey of self-discovery. He would read many self-help books and started to go to lots of events and even a few retreats.

His friends noticed a marked difference in his outlook, and he seemed more content with his life. However, he approached each one with a different mindset.

Despite all the self-development, he continued to face many setbacks.

Anthony told Joanna that he toyed around with a few business ideas. Some were more successful, whilst others were a total disaster.

One particular disastrous idea was when he created an online financial services product which would give greater financial awareness to the mass market.

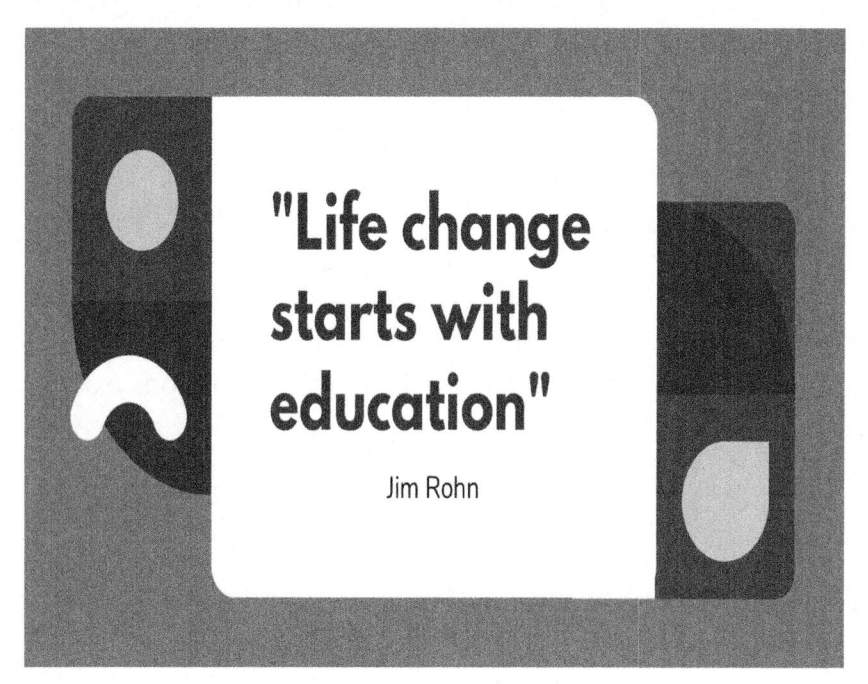

> "Life change starts with education"
> Jim Rohn

Startup Woes

He decided to jump straight into a startup, thinking he could scale it up, sell it, and move on.

Instead, he found himself dealing with lawyers less than one year into a disastrous working relationship with an incompatible business partner who was fresh out of business school.

He had to get rid of the toxic business partner at any cost. The Partner caused him more grief than his clients had ever forced him at Gothman Soanes.

It turned out that the business partner wasn't cut out to be working in a startup.

Despite having an MBA, the Partner had no gravitas, entrepreneurial flair, or skills to manage anything substantial, let alone be trusted to develop and build stakeholder relationships.

Trust Is Fragile

Anthony would also dread when the Partner would speak to people because he feared the worst, especially when the Partner was trying to negotiate and get buy-in from external stakeholders.

Anthony would have to step in repeatedly to finish off the conversations.

He didn't appreciate his Partner's erratic and unprofessional behavior either.

After the product's first iteration, Anthony showed it to potential users, who slated it. Unfortunately, they didn't like the product's design, usability, or functionality.

Anthony felt deflated but relieved because his hunch had come true all along - he no longer trusted his Partner's judgment.

He also learnt an invaluable lesson. He knew he should have spearheaded the project and taken control instead of trusting the Partner, who was good at talking but little else.

Lessons Learnt

One of the biggest lessons Anthony learnt was the following:

"To grow, you must trust the process, especially when you make mistakes."

It would have been easy for Anthony to feel bitter about his past start-up experiences. It turns out he'd been let down, had money stolen from him and ended up with legal issues. Yet you wouldn't have known from the way he talked about it.

Initially, he blamed others but quickly realized he should have been more hands-on and picked the right people.

Dealing With Difficult Conversations

Anthony had a difficult conversation with his Partner, who had mentally exited the project a long time ago. He didn't take the feedback well, and he shouted at Anthony.

If the Partner had been mature and professional enough, he could have been upfront and honest and expressed how he felt. But instead, he chose to step back and do nothing. As a result, Anthony and his Partner reached a stalemate.

Anthony later found out the main reason why the Partner stuck around. He was forwarding his own goals and tail-coating the project to achieve his aims. Anthony thought, "Who the hell does he think he is?

The only way Anthony could move forward was to remove the Partner. So Anthony consulted the lawyers, and the removal of the Partner began in earnest.

The conversation enthralled Joanna. It seemed as if Anthony had been up against it with the start-up compared to Joanna.

Likewise, Anthony knew Joanna understood how setbacks could eventually be a boon instead of a painful scar.

In reality, such setbacks provide ample learning opportunities; there's silver learning in every challenge.

Not Everyone Is Out There To Screw You

He understood Joanna's frustrations because she'd worked hard at the law firm. She was positioning towards a senior promotion, but instead, she found herself back on in the market.

Anthony also tried to reassure Joanna that her redundancy wasn't personal. It was purely a business decision dictated by the economic conditions the States had found themselves dealing with.

He encouraged Joanna to take a step back, assess her options, trust the process, learn from the mistakes, especially the side steps and the rejections and use them to build resilience.

Trust Is Fragile

Anthony learnt about trust the hard way. He found out that the Partner was looking for a free ride and wasn't interested in the business product, market or potential clients.

Towards the end, Anthony discovered the Partner was recording their conversations without his knowledge.

The Partner was also trying to bring on another classmate from B-school by giving him 5% of shareholding but wasn't willing to compromise his share.

Joanna was shocked when she heard about this. How could anyone be so unprofessional? He wanted Anthony to give up 5% shareholding.

Had Anthony accepted, he would have become a minority shareholder in his own company.

Payback is a bitch. Sooner or later, they'd screw over the wrong person. Karma is funny like that.

Lofty business titles didn't matter when there was nothing behind the empty façade.

The conversation with Anthony turned out to be a big eye-opener. She was impressed with the calm manner in which he spoke about the start-up experience.

He didn't feel bitter, nor did he harbor any ill will. He felt the experience gave him a cutting edge when dealing with business.

She admired Anthony for his grit and ability to bounce back and knew he would succeed at whatever venture he pursued.

Expect The Unexpected

Anthony shared some techniques he used to overcome the setbacks along the way.

He mentioned that setbacks were necessary and expected because that's how an individual grows in many cases.

He said many people feared setbacks because they were too worried about what others thought about them.

Ditch Other People's Judgements

Joanna desperately wanted to stop caring what others thought. However, it sounded more straightforward than it was in practice.

Ever since she could remember, she'd considered other people's views, especially her parents, peers, work colleagues, and friends.

Sometimes this would cloud her decision-making process, and more often than she'd like, she chose to follow the advice of others. Anthony said most people do blindly follow others.

Inner Circle Audit

He suggested she write out a personal and professional list of people in her life.

"Joanna, beside each name, write down each person's impact on you. For example, you might think your parents mean well because they are worried you will make mistakes.

However, mistakes are valid because they help you learn and push your experience zones."

"Write it all. When you know the impact your tribe has on you, you'll learn to tune out the negative behavior or energy when it matters.' He elaborated on finding out who your champion was, the energy zapper or the eternal complainer.

"Oh, wow," Joanna hadn't thought about it like that. She just accepted the people in her life for who they were. Like many of her friends and peers, people came into her life or left. Some left a lasting imprint, some positive and some toxic.

She would start to make a mental note of some people that sprung to mind. The first ones were her parents.

Anthony said when you stop caring what others think, you are:

✳ ☐ Mentally free.

✳ ☐ You'll be willing to take opportunities as they present themselves.

✳ ☐ You won't stress too much on the side and back steps because they help you grow.

✳ ☐ You'll be willing to experiment with different ideas.

✳ ☐ You get to write your script.

✳ ☐ You'll feel excited about each day instead of taking each day for granted.

The conversation with Anthony was helping Joanna. She was grateful he'd taken the time to sit with her and help manage her emotions.

Anthony quickly moved on to his next point. Again, she could see his passion as he went from one concept to another.

Receiving A Blank Canvas Each Day

Anthony made a very poignant comment that each of us gets a blank canvas every day. He told her to stop and think about that for a moment.

It was so true. Recently Joanna had been experiencing the same emotions day in and day out.

He said many people don't even think about getting this gift daily. Anthony said he, too, was previously guilty of doing this, and days began to blend into one another, and before he knew it, the week would be over.

He said many people brought yesterday's mindset and baggage to a brand new day, thus impacting the day and choices.

Setting Intentions

Anthony suggested, "Setting the Intention" for the day.

When she woke up these days, the first thing on her mind was getting a job and getting out of this horrible feeling she was experiencing.

She then started thinking about what she needed to do for the day. But, even before getting out of bed, her day was clouded by yesterday's decisions and ideas.

Anthony told her to try the following:

- Don't look at your phone for at least 30 minutes when you wake up.
- Give gratitude for being alive.
- Think about what you want from a brand new day.
- Get out of bed as soon as you hear the alarm. Otherwise, it's too easy to languish in bed and feel sorry for herself.

Ray of Hope

As they continued talking, Joanna could see a ray of hope as she realized that she was the one who could turn her situation around. Her. No one else. That her life and her feelings were placed firmly in her hands.

Joanna recently read 'The Secret'. Even though the Book was top of the charts, she was unimpressed.

The Book talked about how thinking and believing alone would manifest those dreams into reality. She felt this thought process had done a disservice to many people.

Anthony further suggested she take a piece of paper and write out her Career wins and failures.

Career Wins vs. Career Losses

Win 1	Loss 1
Win 2	Loss 2
Win 3	Loss 3

He said this was important to reflect on what had worked and what hadn't.

"Joanna, you can't move forward if your mental baggage takes you back three steps. So it's better to do this work now. You will thank yourself later. Plus, you'll have a more robust platform to build your next steps."

Career SWOT

He then told her to try a career SWOT - Strengths, Weaknesses, Opportunities and Threats.

He proposed she bullet out each section like the example he showed her online.

Anthony suggested tackling the weaknesses first. 'People love to talk about how good they are, but their weaknesses will limit how far they go."

Strengths
What are you doing well? What sets you apart? What are your good qualities?

Weaknesses
Where do you need to improve? Are resources adequate? What do others do better than you?

SWOT ANALYSIS

Opportunities
What are your goals? Are demands shifting? How can it be improved?

Threats
What are the blockers you're facing? What are factors outside of your control?

Then he suggested she focus on the opportunities section a bit more. She could use her daily walks to think of new ideas and add them to her list.

Joanna began to feel very excited as Anthony talked her through the SWOT. She felt hopeful for the first time in a very long time and couldn't wait to go home and act on what they discussed.

As they left, he said, "Joanna, if you need any further help, call me; I'd be happy to help."

She couldn't thank Anthony enough. Finally, someone was holding her accountable and getting her to take action instead of trying to make her feel better with band-aid sentiments.

She wasn't looking to Anthony for all the answers; she wanted someone like him to act as a sounding board.

She was now ready to face the challenges ahead and take control of her situation.

She realized she had more control than she thought. However, it now needed a mindset shift to help her move from being in the passenger seat into the driving seat.

Time to go back to the drawing board.

> SELF-AWARENESS IS A COMPETITIVE TOOL IN THE 21st CENTURY.
>
> Pervin Shaikh

CHAPTER 5

ADJUSTING TO THE NEW NORMAL

After a couple of months, Joanna began taking each day as it came. She started to find her rhythm and felt more optimistic than before.

However, she had low moments on some days, but she had learnt to manage her emotions better.

She knew avoiding the negative thoughts was futile because they played mind games with her.

They would catch up with her when she least expected, and it would take a long time to get back to feeling on top of them.

She changed her approach to her challenges.

Instead of spending lots of time reviewing the same mental script, she learnt to incorporate some fun activities into her day.

She restructured her days and would start with her development work, then job-hunting, and she even managed to find time to squeeze her friends in.

She also tried to keep weekends free to do nice things like going to Central Park, The Met and art galleries scattered around the city.

Her days were filled up with activities that led to better well-being.

She felt a sense of accomplishment.

More importantly, she was channeling her worries, which weren't so intense in frequency as they had been.

Journal Entry

An entry from Joanna's journal highlighted how far she had come.

> Today felt really good because I took control from the start as I've been putting into practice the "Setting the Intentions for the Day" technique that Anthony shared with me.
>
> I like the structure it gives my day because it makes me feel as if I have a bit of control. I want to let God and the universe know what I want from the day. Before I even get out of my bed, I will say a little prayer, and intention and as I put a foot to the ground I've started saying "It's going to be a great day".
>
> I feel more happier and even though the upbeat mood might not last for the whole day, I feel optimistic about my opportunities and I am more willing to explore other avenues.
>
> However, when I tried it yesterday, it was a bit of "hit and miss", because the phone rang and it was the headhunter and they were trying to get me to see Clark and Bane in Manhattan later this week.
>
> I've learnt not to get too upset if my day runs ahead of me. Instead, I'm learning not to beat myself up with my self talk.

Wins today

- Completed my job hunting tasks early this morning
- Reached out to five new companies via LinkedIn
- Networked with five people from university who work in those companies
- Read an article on self branding - this was a very good article which elaborated on building your brand on social media.
- I decided to call my parents and it was good to talk to them. I'm planning to see them next weekend and it will be good for me

What wasn't so good

- I worked very hard on the applications last week and received three rejections today. Bit tough but as the saying goes, when one door closes another ten open.
- The professional indemnity insurance renewal came through today - that's another few hundred bucks.
- I had a little low moment in the afternoon. I just felt like the job hunt is a long grind.
- The job hunt is taking much longer than I thought and trying to stay upbeat is proving to be difficult.
- Law applications are so long and laborious that I don't feel the passion anymore.

I know my heart is not in it and I've known this for a while, but did nothing about it. However, I'm very certain about it now - Law Is Not My thing.

Starting Over Again

As she put her diary away, Joanna started thinking about what else she could do.

She'd been reading about ex-corporate professionals who left their high-powered jobs. Many were rethinking their priorities.

Could Joanna go solo and pursue her dreams? Was she naïve? How would she even go about it?

She realized that the uncertainty around her was the new normal and that what worked yesterday wouldn't serve her well today or tomorrow.

She was nevertheless willing to put in the effort just like Anthony suggested and see how far she could go.

Whenever she reached a mindset milestone, she was faced with further steps into the unknown, but the mountain no longer felt insurmountable.

The New Normal Routine

The new normal had allowed her to start afresh and do what she always wanted: set up her own business. However, she knew this would be very challenging, considering she had no business experience.

Once she did the Career SWOT, she took one of the ideas from the opportunities section and actioned it quickly.

She needed to act sooner before procrastination got the better of her.

She seemed to be excited about a couple of the options. Both were long shots, but Joanna knew it was time to overhaul her career.

She thought about setting up an off-boarding company explicitly working with the legal sector. She could set this up and recruit people to run it for her.

Her second idea, which she was most keen on, was to provide a one-stop 'shop' for burnt-out legal professionals. She knew what was missing from the market because she hadn't found anything that could help legal professionals who wanted out of the profession.

Plan to Succeed

Joanna created two action plans rather than jumping headfirst into the new plan. One was her short-term goals, which would involve getting some contract or freelance work to help her with her finances.

It would also give her more time to fine-tune her long-term goals. So she wrote a new mantra, "Dream It and Do It".

She printed this out and put it on her desk at eye level.

She used an iPad to create an idea board, and soon her screen was covered with a bunch of virtual post-it notes in different colors.

She set about creating stretch goals, and after each day and week, she would undertake a daily evaluation exercise. She asked herself the following questions:

✽ ☐ What worked?

* ☐ What wasn't so good?

* ☐ What could be better?

After just two weeks, she noticed a marked difference and decided to carry on with this exercise each day. She appreciated the power of consistency which led to momentum.

Joanna noticed her interactions with others had changed too. Finally, she became more confident in the way she interacted with others.

She met with Adriana and Tara at Sey Coffee in Bushwick, East Williamsburg. She met both at college; it had been ages since they last met. Both saw a noticeable change in Joanna.

"How's it going, Joanna"? Both were curious to find out what Joanna was going to do next.

Joanna sensed the competitive streak coming out of Tara, but Joanna had known them long enough to know that the competition between the three was healthy.

Adriana and Tara both worked in big law firms in NYC and seemed to be successful in their careers.

Joanna mentioned she was applying to companies, but the market was challenging. She didn't say anything about the personal development she was doing daily.

Unlearn to Relearn

When she first embarked on the journey, Joanna thought what she had previously learnt from her old world would help her move forward to the new world she found herself in.

However, the old rule book of school and grades wasn't enough to help her. Instead, to move forward, she would need the right mindset and tools to navigate an uncertain business world. Anthony was right all along.

The era of DIY Learning was upon them, and Joanna appreciated the importance of keeping experience, skills and knowledge updated.

Sometimes, she found that when she was highly critical of herself, she felt pressured to make decisions and sometimes not the right ones.

Other times, when she was kinder to herself and nurtured her inner and outer self

She wanted to set goals and make ambitious plans because she had the mind space to do so.

Joanna wanted to get better at learning new things without being critical of her old learning style.

She saw an infographic on Twitter which caught her eye. It was straightforward. Learn, Unlearn, Relearn. She liked it.

Joanna saw the thinking behind it. It's essential to learn, unlearn when the learning no longer serves you, and relearn to replace outdated knowledge.

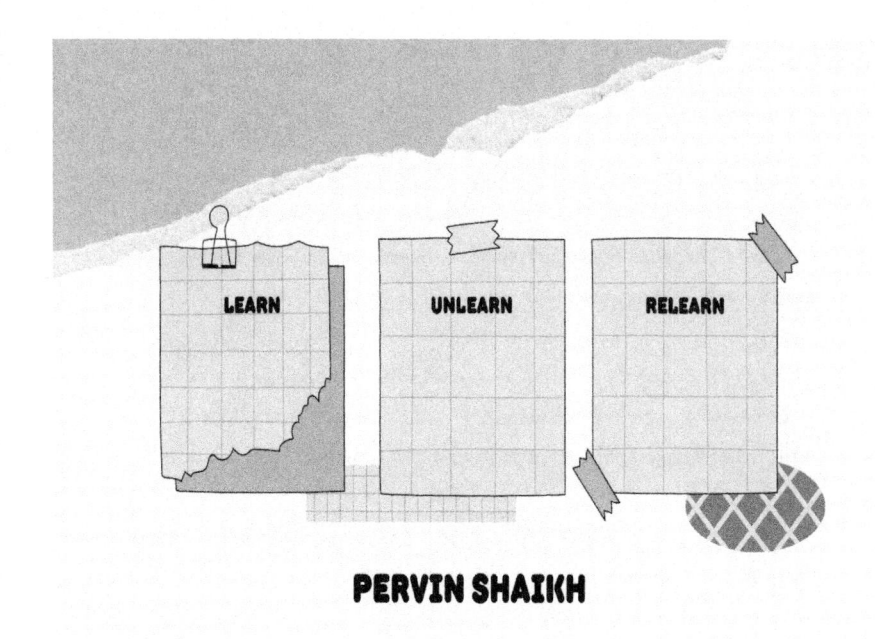

Journal Your Way To Success

Joanna made a point of journaling every day.. She found it helped her deal reflect on her day.

It also helped her process the challenges. She noticed her learning came when she started asking the right questions.

She made a note of the insights in her journal:

Today was a bit more challenging because there was so much going on. I'm glad I didn't pursue Clark & Bane. They were keen to meet again but I informed the headhunter that six months would be too long for me. They didn't want someone for three months which could have worked.

Thankfully, I've got some freelance work with Blume who is a start-up legal company which hires lawyers as per client project need. The work started off slow, but has picked up post the pandemic.

The way it works is when a start-up contacts them, Blume selects three lawyers and sends the clients their profiles.

The client can choose one lawyer to speak to with for a 15 minute no fee exploratory conversation. The lawyer then sends the brief plus estimated cost of the work. If the client is happy, Blume takes a percentage.

I want to move ahead with my business ideas too. Working with Blume has showed me that my model could work too. I like this model and might think about it for my own commercial projects.

Recap

✳ ☐ Be kind to yourself.

✳ ☐ Manage your expectations.

✳ ☐ Setting goals will help achieve the desired results.

✳ ☐ It's ok to make mistakes. Just don't beat yourself up about it.

✳ ☐ Keep a journal to capture your thoughts and learning.

✳ ☐ Take time to do other things.

Possibilities Are Endless With The Right Mindset

Joanna increased her learning and development as she adjusted to the new normal. She also approached her job hunt differently. She was still looking for a full-time role but also explored contracting and freelance work.

She recently signed with Fiverr.com and offered her legal services to companies on a project-by-project basis.

Who knows, maybe Joanna could secure other work on the Fiverr.com platform and do this for a little while.

Feast and Famine Cycle

Joanna knew lawyers could charge a lot of money, but when she secured some work at Blume, she appreciated her hourly financial potential.

However, although it was lucrative, she knew freelancing was never stable. Plus, it was cyclical too.

Anthony told her about the 'Feast and Famine Cycle', which was true.

There would be some months when hectic and others when it was very quiet. Anthony usually used these quiet months to work on new projects.

If Joanna were to build a portfolio career, she would also need to assess other areas of her life. She had started thinking about giving up her spacious Williamsburg apartment, but she still had some time on her lease contract.

For the time being, she decided to focus on developing her business ideas in-between dealing with clients.

Shaking It Up A Bit

When she worked in the office, she had ample opportunities to walk into the partner's office and discuss an idea.

However, she didn't have anyone she could do this with at home. She tried some FB networking groups, but it wasn't her thing.

Even when the pandemic was over, and Joanna went to a face-to-face networking event, she felt it was too salesy. Many people were in the same predicament as Joanna and were doing what newbies do: try convincing the wrong audience.

She also came away with more business cards than when she worked in the law firm. She decided to ditch the networking and find her tribe.

Find Your Champions

Anthony was the one she knew who was great at expanding his network, involving people from all walks of life. He said he built it up over the years and told her the golden rule of networking - Network without expectations.

He said many people made a rookie mistake by asking for help in the first interaction.

He categorically stated that was a big no-no because you haven't built any leverage with the contact.

He also highlighted a critical point. People buy people based on trust. If you haven't built trust with someone, why would they be willing to help you?

He suggested she start with a couple of people and add to her network just as she did on LinkedIn. He told her to build a relationship in the first instance and, instead of asking, try and see where Joanna could add value to them.

How could Joanna build her tribe? Most of her friends were still working in the corporate world and weren't suitable anyway.

Keyboard Warrior Fatigue

It was all too easy to sit behind a keyboard and try to build bridges with people.

Joanna was finding networking difficult. Initially, she dealt with various emotions, including loneliness, anxiety and bewilderment.

So she decided to mix up her working day.

Some days she would go down to the coffee shop. Other times she would go to downtown Manhattan and find places there.

She enjoyed varying her routine because it shifted her perspective and helped her look at some of her challenges in a new light.

CHAPTER 6

PRODUCTIVITY

Joanna was beginning to feel a bit better, not to mention stronger, with each passing day. Anthony had been right about her progress.

She attributed her renewed energy to a combination of exercise and journaling.

The former strengthened her body, the latter, her mind.

Writing her thoughts down on paper helped her self-reflect.

She had a better understanding of what she wanted and how she could go about getting it.

When she walked into the gym that day, it was practically deserted. Maybe it had something to do with the long weekend.

Regardless, Joanna was there and ready to rock.

About halfway through her workout, she happened to see Anthony walk in. She smiled, hoping to catch his eye, but someone walked in front of her just as he came in.

Anthony disappeared, so Joanna assumed he popped into the locker room to get changed.

Fifteen minutes later, she heard his voice from behind her. "Taking it easy on yourself today, I see." Joanna cracked a smile and turned around.

"Just pacing myself." Which wasn't true, as her shirt could attest to.

She continued, "It's good to see you again. I wanted to thank you for your tips. They made all the difference. Got any more?

Summary

"Now that you have some momentum, I think it's time to talk productivity," Anthony said as he sat down to do some sit-ups.

"A big part of productivity is your health; thankfully, you're way ahead of the game there." He continued, "Health is the first layer of productivity, and people often ignore it the most. People focus on finding ways to do more because they think that's where the answer lies."

"That's so me," Joanna thought to herself. She had put in long hours ever since she joined her firm. Her family had taught her never to be afraid of a little hard work.

Back in her school days, her parents reminded her over and over again of the importance of studying.

It had become ingrained in her, so even after graduating, she continued to believe that the harder she worked, the better off she'd be.

Anthony continued, "Most people confuse activity with productivity. Activity is easy. Anyone can work hard.

Most people do. But successful people know it's not just about working hard but a combination of hard work and implementing the four layers of productivity.

Once they learn to tap into all four layers, they start to make quantum leaps in their success."

"Four?"

"Yes," Anthony reached into his gym bag, pulled out a piece of paper and a pen, and scribbled out a triangle.

Then he drew three lines cutting the triangle into four distinct layers, labeling the bottom one HEALTH.

"As I mentioned earlier, health is the foundation."

"What are the other three?"

Anthony wrote HABITS, PERSONAL DEVELOPMENT and STRATEGIES in the remaining layers. He then drew a line around the triangle and labeled it TECHNOLOGY.

"Tech isn't a layer but can enhance each triangle area when applied correctly." When it was done, it looked like this:

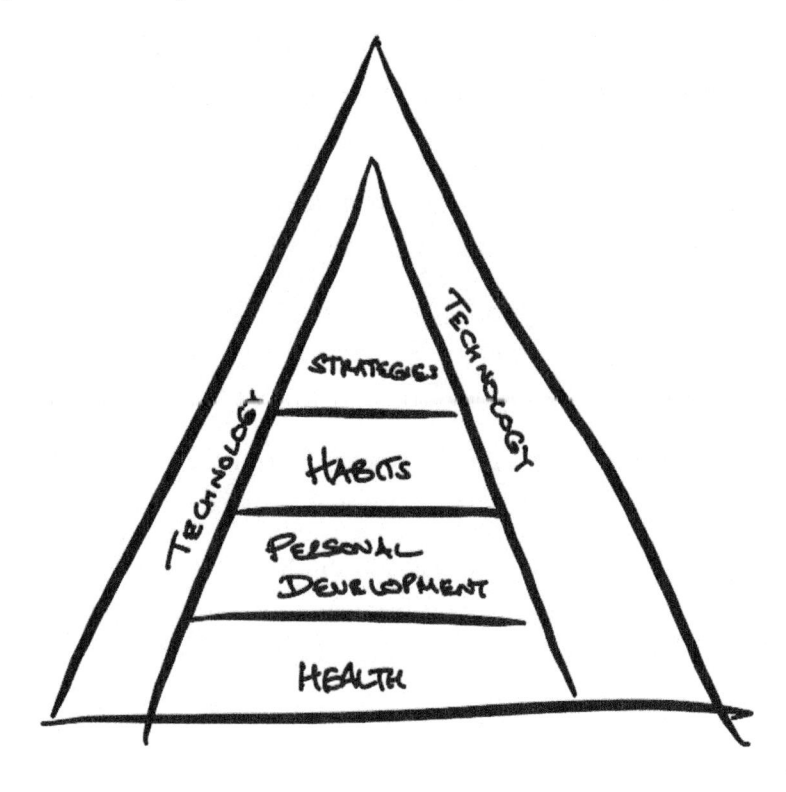

The Productivity Pyramid

"Looks like I've got my work cut out for me," Joanna said, looking at the triangle.

Habits and strategies seemed rather elementary. Joanna was sure she could probably pick up a book or two on Amazon later related to them, but PERSONAL DEVELOPMENT stood out to her.

"How does personal development fit in when it comes to productivity?"

Personal Development

"My mentor once told me, 'You can only be as productive as you feel.' Health is about developing a strong physique. It has the strength to do what is needed." He flexed his right arm, not in a show-offy way but someone proud of themselves.

"Personal development, on the other hand, is all about this." Tapping the side of his forehead.

"We must develop our mind just like we do our body. Our mindset acts as an amplifier of sorts with everything we do. In many ways, it's like tech for our mind."

"Can you give me an example?" Joanna asked.

"It might be best to share a few quotes from one of my mentors and then see what you make of them."

A sherpa. Anthony was not much of a teacher; he was more of a guide. He liked to share stories, quotes and anecdotes and let people figure things out for themselves.

It was the old teach-a-man-to-fish principle, and Joanna appreciated that.

"Ok, let me have them."

Anthony finished doing his reps, wiped his forehead, and picked up his phone. He clicked the Pages app and opened a file aptly entitled Jim Rohn.

"Ok, let me find it." He scrolled down a few pages, then said, "Aha, there it is." Joanna was all ears.

"This is what Jim Rohn calls the best-kept secret of the rich. Here goes – 'Rich people have about…24 hours a day.'"

Joanna was waiting for Anthony to finish the story, but Anthony put his phone down and just looked at her.

"Is that it?"

Anthony nodded.

Joanna was at a loss. Of course, rich people have 24 hours a day. We all have 24 hours a day. Whether you're American, French or Japanese, male or female, tall or short, slender or fat, 1440 minutes a day is all we get.

Anthony could see Joanna was somewhat frustrated, so he added, "You seem disappointed."

"Well, if I'm sincere, yes." Not wanting to offend him.

"I get it. I remember when I first heard it. I mean, it's pretty straightforward, isn't it?"

Joanna nodded.

Anthony continued, "Let me tell you a story that might help you make sense of it.

When I was a child, I was traveling in the Philippines with my family, and one Sunday, we were out for a drive when we came across a beautiful waterfall.

What was remarkable was you could get on a raft and go under the waterfall for a small fee. Even as a kid, I found it breathtaking.

I begged my parents to take me on it. There wasn't a long wait, so about 10 minutes later, we set off on the little bamboo raft heading towards the waterfall.

My heart was pounding with excitement. However, the closer we got to the waterfall, the louder it became. You could hear its incredible power.

My excitement turned to fear. As we started going under the waterfall, it felt like I was getting pounded on my head with tens of blows.

The pressure was incredible. The sound of the water muffled my screams. Thankfully, it only took a few seconds to make it into the cave behind the waterfall. Unfortunately, we had to go back through. My parents did what they could to cover for me, but it still hurt.

Then, it was all over. The warm sun on my face dried my tears.

I've never forgotten that experience, even though it happened almost 40 years ago.

What I realized later is that water is very much like time. Concentrated, it can generate incredible force, but most of the time, people see water as just something beautiful or refreshing. They don't understand its true power."

Joanna thought for a second and then said, "So what your mentor wanted to impress on people is that though rich people have the same amount of time as everyone else, they're doing something different with it."

Anthony nodded. "Jim Rohn, in all his lectures, would also say, 'Learn to work harder on yourself than you do on your job.'"

That hit Joanna hard. All her life, she'd worked hard, but it was always for a grade, a salary or a promotion, and as a result, she'd overlooked herself.

She had to admit that the past few weeks were the first time she had put herself first. It all began with her decision to go to the gym regularly.

She was feeling better both physically and mentally. The changes had taken effect rather quickly.

She also started noticing the two types of people in society–those who prioritizing health and those who do not. Walking around the park or on the city streets, it wasn't hard to tell.

Joanna had started realizing that one's shopping cart reflected the person pushing it.

Ever since she started going to the gym, she has been cooking more and, as a result, eating healthier and drinking more water.

Gone were the days of a few glasses of wine with dinner, as was so often the case when she worked alongside her colleagues.

But that was just the start of her transformation. Journaling gave her a better understanding of what she wanted and acted as a road map moving forward.

"Personal development is all about being the best you can be," Anthony said. "Physically, mentally and spiritually. Your company is not in charge of that; you are. It's only when I learnt that my life changed."

Habits

"So, what about the next level up? Habits," Joanna asked.

"Habits are what solidify and automate your newfound knowledge. Too many people go all gung-ho when they 'discover' personal development. They spend eight hours in the gym trying to get in shape and inevitably fizzle out. It's what I like to call the New Year's conundrum.

Every year, millions of people like to make grand resolutions to get in shape, stop wasting money, eat less, drink less, spend more time with their kids, etc. The first two weeks of January gyms are packed. Many people do try and stay true to their word.

But come the end of January, the gyms are quiet. Most people have given up. Their resolutions are a distant memory. They say to themselves, 'There's always next year.' And they're right. They forget that for the next 11 months, they have just waved the white flag at."

It was almost as if most people treated their New Year's resolutions as nothing more than empty promises we made to ourselves to sound good. Joanna thought about all the times she and her friends had failed with their resolutions. She'd lost count.

Anthony could see Joanna was processing what he had said.

"Habits make up roughly 40% of our lives. Our minds don't want to work hard, so they do their best to make things easy for us. Habits achieve this. The problem is not all habits are good. Just the opposite, most habits, unless actively created, are negative."

"What do you mean negative?"

"Every day when people come home from work, people open a bottle of wine and turn on Netflix, or sit on the couch and surf Instagram. These habits help us unwind after a hard work day, but these are default habits. They weren't created through any effort.

Instead of watching Netflix, read a good book. Instead of drinking a bottle of wine, which dehydrates you, make yourself a green smoothie instead of surfing Insta or journal. These habits take effort, but since habits take up such a big part of our daily lives, you want to have as many positive habits as possible.

I'm not saying give up everything you enjoy. You can still watch Netflix; limit how much time you spend on it. TikTok, Instagram, Twitter and YouTube are designed to keep you there. It's not for your benefit, but theirs. It's up to you to limit their effect on you."

She thought about all the bad habits she'd picked up over the years. The late nights, the midnight snacks, the lack of exercise, the fast food, the hours spent mindlessly scrolling on social media, the celebrity gossip, skipping breakfast, the six-dollar-double-milk Frappuccinos. They all added up.

"40%," she thought to herself. It hadn't dawned on her that much of her life, and everyone else's, was dominated by habits.

She might never have even noticed if Anthony had not mentioned it, but now it was crystal clear.

"Ok, I'm with you. What habits are worth creating?" Joanna asked.

"That's not for me to decide. However, everything started to change after I made reading a habit."

"Reading?" Joanna seemed puzzled.

"Education is where change begins. Remember, you have to nourish the body and the mind. Food for the body, knowledge for the mind."

Joanna remembered how one of the partners in her office had a different book on his desk practically every time she went there. He was also the youngest partner the firm ever had. Guess he knew something other people didn't.

"Any suggestions on where to start?"

"Tell you what, I'll send over a list later on."

Strategies

Joanna seemed lost in thought, but Anthony's voice brought her back to reality.

"Ten," he huffed. Beads of sweat were dripping down his face.

He reached for his towel and proceeded to wipe his face dry. After catching his breath, he said, "Once you have those habits in place, it's time to ramp things up a notch with strategies. These can still work without the first two levels, but they won't be as effective as being used on top of them." Anthony said as he sat down to do a few more reps.

Joanna was about to say something but decided to keep quiet. Instead, she started thinking about what productivity strategies she had learnt in the past and if she had stopped using them.

She remembered being taught the 80/20 rule back by one of her professors in college and found it rather intriguing.

"Like the 80/20 rule?" she asked.

Anthony had just finished another set of reps and was cooling himself down. He looked at her and said, "That's a good place to start. Tell me what you know about it."

"Errr…" Joanna felt caught off-balance.

"Well, if I remember correctly, it states that 80% of our outcomes come from 20% of our efforts and visa-versa."

"Which means?" Anthony queried.

"We need to focus our energies on that 20%," Joanna answered.

Anthony nodded but then added, "And?"

Joanna wasn't sure what he wanted her to say.

After a few seconds of silence, Anthony gave her a masterclass on the 80/20 rule in less than a minute.

"The 80/20 rule was created by an Italian economist Vilfrado Pareto in the early 1900s. He discovered it while looking at pea pods in his garden, if you can believe that. Since then, it's been applied to everything from land ownership to clothing use to investments and habits. However, most people don't know how to unleash its full power.

The 80/20 can be reapplied to itself. Done so, you'll find that 64% of your outcomes are obtained from 4% of your activity.

Reapplied, you'll see that 1% of what you do gets you 51% of your results. That means

Your single, most important goal is to determine what 1% of activities are and do them."

Joanna looked stunned. Anthony could tell she was absorbing what he had just said. It seemed apparent when he said it, but no one had ever told her. She ran over all her accounts, problems, mistakes, stress, and relationships. She had to admit that in nearly every case, when you got right down to the bottom, there was one single issue that accounted for a large part of it.

"Damn," she said out loud. Though she was still processing Anthony's upgraded 80/20 concept, she couldn't help but ask, "What else?"

Anthony could spend hours talking about time management, but as he had another appointment, he said, "Tell you what, tonight after you get home, take about an hour and research time management strategies. Write down the ones that stick out to you, and I'll take a look at them next time we meet." Anthony looked at his watch.

Technology

That sounded good to her. After all, Anthony had already been so generous with his time. He'd shown her the path; now it was time for her to take the reins.

"One quick question about the pyramid. Why's technology not at the top?" Joanna asked.

"Technology acts as a sort of support system. It helps make things easier for us. I can remember a time before all these gadgets we take for granted today: no iPhones, no Airpods, no Alexa, no nothing. Yet we got by just fine. Slow, but OK.

Technology has changed how we live our lives, but not in the way most people think. We still do very much what we used to do, except faster, more efficiently and much more quickly.

It feels like every week, new apps and software are being released, promising to speed up every aspect of their lives. The problem today isn't finding technology but finding good software for our unique situation."

Joanna remembered that two years after she had first joined the firm, they had changed the software to "facilitate better lines of communication and increase productivity." The shift had caused all sorts of trouble. It got so bad that after using it for six months, it was scrapped, and things went back to how they were.

"Tech is a double-edged sword," Anthony said as he took off his gloves and put them in his gym bag.

"Tech can enhance our productivity many times over. We can set up apps to deal with so much of our business and private lives, freeing up more valuable time for ourselves. However, we'll waste our' new-found' time if we don't have the rest of the pyramid."

Joanna liked it when he used air quotes.

"What about those who aren't tech savvy? Doesn't tech cause more problems for them?"

"There was a time when you could fight technology, but look at what's in your hand."

She looked down and saw her phone.

"That little device changed everything. At one-time, tech was limited to office space and homes. Today, it's everywhere. You can't fight it. The answer to your question is yes, but that's how it is. It's here to stay, and either you learn to use it, or you don't and get left behind."

And with that, Anthony wiped his forehead, put his phone in his bag, and apologized. He wanted to stay, but as he said, 'I've got one of that 1% I need to attend to."

That evening on the way home, Joanna's mind was buzzing. She was thinking about the pyramid and wondered why no one had ever mentioned it. She thought it seemed like something they should teach in a school or at least in college.

She'd graduated from a prestigious college, costing her a small fortune in the process, yet none of her professors had ever mentioned this simple concept.

As she walked into her apartment that evening, her phone buzzed. It was from Anthony.

As promised, he had sent her a list of 20 books with two highlighted. She sat in front of her MacBook, opened up Amazon and added them to her wish list. She added to her shopping cart all except the two he had highlighted. "There's no time like the present," she thought and hit purchase.

She had work to do.

Anthony's List of Books

1. *Rich Dad, Poor Dad* by Robert Kiyosaki
2. *How to Win Friends and Influence People* by Dale Carnegie
3. *The Four-Hour Work Week* by Tim Ferriss
4. *The 7 Habits of Highly Effective People* by Stephen Covey
5. *The Ride of a Lifetime* by Robert Iger
6. *Awaken the Giant Within* by Anthony Robbins
7. *He Can Who Thinks He Can* by Orison Swett Marson
8. *The Tao of Warren Buffett* by Mary Buffett
9. *The 5 Major Pieces of the Life Puzzle* by Jim Rohn
10. *The Compound Effect* by Darren Hardy
11. *Shoe Dog* by Phil Knight
12. *Extreme Ownership* by Jocko Willink
13. *The Purple Cow* by Seth Godin
14. *Body and Soul* by Anita Roddick
15. *The Third Door* by Alex Banayan
16. *The 48 Laws of Power* by Robert Greene
17. *Free to Focus* by Michael Hyatt
18. *Thick Face, Black Heart* by Chin-Ning Chu
19. *The Snowball Effect* by Kristin Barton Cuthriell M.Ed
20. *The Lessons of History* by Will Durant

CHAPTER 7

CREATING THE RIGHT ENVIRONMENT

Like many people, Joanna struggled with the new world during the pandemic. On the one hand, she was a little ahead of the others when dealing with and adapting to change, but working from home required an altogether different mindset and approach.

Luckily, she had met Anthony recently, who helped her see workplace changes in a new light.

She remembered what he said that the pandemic had cemented what was already in motion - hybrid working. Technology has allowed people to work from anywhere, something Tim Ferriss discussed in his book *The 4-Hour Work Week*.

Anthony had worked from home for a few years now, and he enjoyed the freedom of being in control of his time.

He said he got more done because he didn't have office distractions. But most people hadn't been in a position to be able to do that.

However, the pandemic changed all that.

With employees being forced to work from home, Anthony knew most would ask to make this part of their working routine. He referred to it as "The Shift".

The old way of working was well and truly over. Technology made it possible. In this new world, people could work more or less wherever and whenever.

When it came to Joanna maximizing her working-from-home experience, he provided excellent support in helping her make working from home a big success.

What she liked about Anthony's approach was the way he supported her. Fortunately, for Joanna's sake, he didn't give Joanna all the answers.

Working From Home

Like countless others, Joanna tried several different approaches as she adjusted to Working From Home (WFH); some of those practices worked, whilst others were a total disaster.

Despite all the good intentions and plans, there would be days when she would get very little done and feel guilty for not being productive enough.

Early on, the distractions got the best of her. Before she knew it, Joanna's well-intended plans got waylaid for another day.

There was a danger that days would have turned into weeks if she continued, and if she were not careful, a month would have flown by.

She found some of the distractions particularly frustrating, especially if someone was calling her on her mobile or she'd receive an unexpected email or even friends setting up Zoom calls for a "quick chat", which turned into hours.

During the lockdown, it had been even worse.

Joanna's schedule would be very tight when she started job hunting and worked as a contractor from home.

She needed to be diligent in creating a weekly plan. However, there was no wriggle room if there was a schedule change.

Changes in her schedule were the leading cause of frustration because there was no buffer in her daily plan. It meant she'd be carrying tasks over to the next day, which led to increased anxiety.

Maybe it was time Joanna stopped the 'should, would and could' and focused on trying different ways of working.

Joanna started experimenting with different schedules and allowed a bit more buffer time in the week. She breathed easy as the plan was more fluid.

Discipline is doing what you need to do, whether you feel like it or not.
Adrian Shepherd

She started getting more disciplined after a few initial hiccups.

Instead of working anywhere and everywhere in her Williamsburg apartment, she decided to find a suitable space in her spacious apartment and make that her dedicated "office space."

It worked so well for her that she decided to do the same if she ever moved.

Joanna kept her working space solely for work purposes, even when she wasn't working.

She kept her laptop and iPad in one place, so there was no temptation to sprawl her work all over the apartment, which she did when she first started.

Now able to move about again, she decided to work a couple of days at a coffee shop on the Upper West Side.

That way, she was unlikely to bump into anyone she knew.

Find The Best Method For You

Anthony encouraged Joanna to find her strategies and processes. He said what worked for him might not work for her or anyone else.

In essence, we need to personalize our approach to work.

Phew! Joanna was relieved. It took the pressure off of molding herself into someone else's routine, which always happened in the corporate world.

She had tried to emulate Patrick at work many times, but she found it challenging to keep up the momentum.

More importantly, Joanna understood why it didn't feel good because it wasn't her style.

She saw others in the workplace do it, too, especially aspiring professionals trying to fit in.

She'd seen Zach in Corporate Development do it. He was the law firm's golden boy and a solid C-Suite contender.

Both Zach and Patrick were corporate men. Zach was a natural networker who seemed to know many people in and out of the Company.

His behavior and mannerisms were so corporate, and when he spoke, he was a carbon copy of Patrick.

They both looked and walked the part and were very polished too. Zach looked content on its surface, and Joanna often wondered if Zack was happy underneath the corporate face.

Trial and Error

Joanna tried different techniques so she could find a happy medium. Initially, it took a little while to find her rhythm, especially if she was working away from home.

Most days, she seemed to get a lot done, but the tasks felt so cumbersome on some days.

It was easier to try different routines at home because she could get up, do her morning routine, and start working at a set time.

She tried to keep a workday schedule, especially as it allowed her to focus on tasks requiring greater concentration.

Working outside in a local coffee shop or hotel required more planning. Joanna needed to leave home early to secure the best spots in most cases.

If she turned up at 10 am, the early birds had taken all her favorite places.

It would then take a bit of emotional energy to fire up the cylinders by 11 am. Joanna also tried to avoid the rush hour.

Even though Joanna had taken two doses of the Pfizer vaccine, she wasn't comfortable traveling on busy trains.

Joanna tried to leave by 4 pm. So in effect, she had 5 hours of work to complete.

Making The Bed

However, there was one thing Joanna did religiously - change out of her pajamas and make the bed each morning.

She'd watched a YouTube Video of a graduation speech given by Admiral McRaven, an ex-Navy Seal and she felt pumped after watching it.

He advocated making the bed first thing in the morning. It starts your day off with a win, which you'll be able to enjoy at the end of it. That would be the first accomplishment of the day.

Once the bed was made, other accomplishments of the day were achievable.

Trying Different Places

After the pandemic, when restrictions were lifted, she found many people doing the same as Joanna - Going to local coffee shops to work. However, there were times when she felt it was too crowded, too cold/hot, noisy with young mothers and strollers, or construction work was going on.

Initially, she would tolerate the external noise and try to carry on. However, it would affect her concentration levels and her mood. Instead of getting work done, her work mood and pattern got impacted by others.

She decided to invest in a pair of Airpod Pros to tune out the external noise. The noise canceling function was a godsend and allowed her to work uninterrupted for her 90-minute jams that Anthony had suggested.

Now, when she didn't like the place's vibe, she learnt to move elsewhere quickly instead of tolerating it and trying to work in a challenging environment. She learnt to adjust her plans and go with the flow.

The post-corporate Joanna was less tolerant of external distractions and felt comfortable adapting quickly. Adapting to changing environments helped her build resilience and not take things personally.

For example, instead of losing her cool at the screaming toddler or the mother for disturbing her space, she would calmly get up and move elsewhere without fanfare.

Just because Joanna was working and engrossed in her work, it didn't mean to say she would expect others to respect her need for some quiet time. After all, other people had the right to enjoy public space, too.

Joanna decided to find three new places to work in her area, and then she had one in downtown Manhattan.

She recently took out a membership at a local cultural center with great views of Hudson Bay.

However, it took an hour to get to; thus, Joanna would only go once a week if she had a lighter day in her schedule.

She used this space for creative thinking, journaling, learning and self-development.

She decided to use the local places to do more serious work like job hunting.

Consistency Leads To Results

Joanna was quick to appreciate that change was part of the growth process.

She understood that she would have to trust the steps to grow, especially those leading her sideways and backwards.

These steps were the most frustrating because she wanted results – fast.

She remembered Anthony's words very vividly. "Master patience, and you master the game."

He said many people don't appreciate the way change works.

He said amateurs always expect instant results, in contrast to getting instant feedback from school, workplace and peers.

However, it was necessary to remember that results didn't miraculously manifest overnight because that's not how change works.

It's a slow process but a necessary one. Anthony told her the process could take weeks, months, and sometimes years for the best results.

Joanna struggled with patience, especially in the corporate world where everything was urgent and wanted yesterday.

Speed was the game's name in the corporate world, where results mattered. Period.

At work, she knew some of those deadlines might have seemed critical at the time, but they came at the expense of physical and mental well-being.

Joanna still adopted the corporate mindset after she left the law firm, especially during her job hunt, but she quickly realized that things took time.

She would need to approach change like a marathon runner and not a sprinter. So she was slowly learning to embrace patience.

Joanna likened her experience to that of a germinating seed. Once the seed was planted, it took a while to show some physical change above the soil level.

The hard work began underneath the soil level, and a more robust foundation was built for the seed to germinate.

Joanna knew she was changing every day, too, and over time, the growth helped her with the next steps.

In the beginning, she expected miracles when she'd completed all the tasks and waited for the fruits of her labor, but she would have to wait a bit longer.

Sharing The Experiences

As Joanna experimented with different approaches, she would journal the pros and cons of each one.

She also felt she could share her highs and lows with Anthony if she needed further help.

When she became comfortable, she started relying on her journal to work through ideas, setbacks and issues.

Her earlier posts seem childish because she was adjusting to a new way of processing information.

The early days felt like a rollercoaster with many challenges and often from different and unexpected areas in quick succession of each other, and usually all on the same day.

Anthony, however, was very good at helping Joanna identify her distractions. He said the distractions played a significant role in goal achievement.

The Dreaded Buzz

Joanna had discovered her distractors with a bit of trial and error. The ones that side-tracked her the most were her mobile notifications.

With over ten apps actively notifying her, she found she subconsciously reached out for her phone whenever she received a message or felt a buzz.

In the beginning, Joanna didn't switch off her notifications.

Instead, she decided to do something she would never have dreamed of doing; she left the phone in another room and would only look at her messages at certain times during the day.

She decided FOMO (Fear of Missing Out) wouldn't stop her from switching off the notifications.

The other notifications she needed to watch out for were unexpected phone calls or emails, especially from her folks in California, who wanted to see how she was doing.

These calls could take up to an hour, but it was about managing the post-phone call state of mind after each call.

She knew her folks meant well, but she struggled to deal with their concern for the job hunt situation.

Maybe she could apply some of the techniques from Marie Kondo.

Marie Kondo for Business

Flipping through Netflix one night, she came across a show by the organization-guru Marie Kondo.

She'd heard the name before but never put any faith in it. However, growth had opened Joanna to learning from the most unusual sources, so she decided to give it a shot."

She was impressed with her approach to turning the untidiest homes into beautiful, tidy ones.

The technique might help her focus better, especially when interviewing with companies for short-term contracts, but more importantly, working on her business plan for her big dream project.

Step by step, Joanna learnt to break big goals into smaller ones. She understood how powerful her brain could be, especially when finding solutions to her challenges.

Journal Entry

Today was a perfect day because it was productive, and I spent some time working on my list in the morning. Sam and Anthony had opened my eyes to the power of focus. Anthony suggested I try the Pomodoro technique.

When I focus, I get so much done. Sam always uses the Pomodoro Technique, which involves working for 25 minutes and taking a five-minute break. Repeat it.

I find I can only do a maximum of four times before I find myself losing momentum. I've experimented with different timings as well. If I'm working on longer pieces, I might do a Pomodoro for 40 minutes and take a 10-minute break.

When I'm focused, I can block out the distractions much better, and it helps me get a lot more done and within a set time frame.

I even had time in the evening to meet up with the crew for drinks and nibbles on the rooftop. I'm going to miss these socials when I move, as we've built a friendly community of like-minded friends who've been fun to chill with, especially after the dark days following the redundancy.

Who knows, I might even come back to Williamsburg at a later date, but in my heart, I know I need to move forward.

Tomorrow is another busy day, and I want to make sure I wake up feeling fresh to tackle the work I have ahead of me.

CHAPTER 8

MASTERMIND

Things were looking up for Joanna.

Her regular gym visits not only had her looking better but feeling better as well.

Anthony had labeled health as the foundation of his Productivity Pyramid, and Joanna understood why.

Her newfound energy and vigor were helping her in every area of her life.

There was something both powerful and rewarding about being able to have a better body. Her friends had noticed a change within her as well.

When she ran into Brandon and Matt the other day at the supermarket, they first mentioned how much better she looked.

She wanted to tell them about her journey but didn't want to come off as bragging, so she merely mentioned that she had started going to the gym.

Joanna realized that she had changed. She could see it in the mirror as well as her attitude. Joanna felt in control of her life for the first time in a long time.

She had realized that while she seemed to have everything – a good job, nice perks, the stylish apartment, stays at friendly hotels – she wasn't in control. Instead, she found herself at the mercy of her employer and clients.

She remembered what Matt had told her at the rooftop party a few weeks ago, "Losing my job was the best thing that ever happened to me."

She finally was beginning to understand why he said that.

She wasn't running her own company or had just landed a job she wanted, but she felt a whole lot better.

When she went to the gym later that day, she was eager to share her insight with

Anthony, but he wasn't around. He didn't show up at all that day or the day after.

But when she walked into the gym on Friday, she heard a familiar voice behind her.

"Miss me?" said Anthony.

"Not at all," said Joanna. But it was obvious she was lying.

His smile and confidence were hard to explain, but people seemed to gravitate towards him wherever he was.

Her father called it "Je ne sais quoi", a French term meaning literally, "I don't know what," but commonly used to explain people's intangibles, their ability to get people to like them.

"My kid was sick on Wednesday, so I had to take him to the doctor's." His son was only 12 but had won two medals at the Junior Olympics for swimming.

Anthony explained how vigorous the schedule was, often waking up at 4:30 to take his son to swim practices and attend late-night training. "It takes a toll," he said.

Joanna imagined that Anthony played basketball for his college team, probably where he began to understand the importance of health and its relationship to productivity.

"But enough about me, I've been curious to hear how things have been going with you."

Joanna told him about running into her friends at the supermarket. She also mentioned getting a few callbacks from the resumes she sent out.

More importantly, though, Joanna seemed full of life. The way she spoke, her demeanor, and even how she walked had changed, and it spoke volumes.

"That's great to hear," said Anthony, "Things seem to be falling into place for you." Joanna couldn't help but feel proud.

"You've already come far; I think you're ready for the next lesson. And as it happens, it fits in nicely with my son getting sick."

Your First Mastermind

"Family," said Anthony, "is everything."

Joanna couldn't help but think back to her childhood and her incredible relationship with her parents and siblings.

Sure, they fought at times, but they had always been there for her. They had instilled within her some of the most valuable attributes – hard work, discipline, courage, and faith. Thinking of her family brought a smile to her face.

"Not everyone is as lucky as us, Joanna. I can tell from the smile on your face your family holds a special place in your heart as they do mine.

I've always loved the quote, 'Family are people who know everything about you and still love you.' But when you become a parent, everything changes.

I can't tell you how much my son changed me. The greatest thing he taught me was patience.

Growing up, I'd get frustrated with people when they didn't understand things quickly. My son taught me to dial things back a notch."

Johanna was surprised to hear Anthony had been impatient.

He was one of the calmest people she had ever met. He never got frustrated or angry.

He seemed to always be in control of his emotions, never taking a step out of place.

"I don't think it's too much of a stretch to say that family is often the greatest factor in a person's success."

"But what about people who aren't quite as lucky as us?" Joanna asked.

"Great question. I get a lot of pushback from people when I say how important Family is.

People do great things because of, as well as despite, their families. Families motivate people to do things one way or the other.

I once heard a story of twins being born to an alcoholic father, they followed the twins throughout their lives, and in their late 20s, they interviewed each of them to see how their lives turned out.

The first son had turned out to be an alcoholic, and when asked why his life turned out that way, he replied, 'What do you expect?

Look at my father.' look at my father.' They then interviewed the second son, who had a good job, a lovely young wife and a child. They asked him the same question, and he answered, 'What do you expect?'

One had used his father as an excuse for his life. The other had used his father as inspiration for his life."

Anthony continued, "Family influences us in more ways than we realize, especially when we're young. But as we get older, we need a new family."

Your New Support System

Joanna thought Anthony would ask her why she wasn't married yet, something she dreaded to hear. But what he said next surprised her.

"I'm not talking about getting married and having a kid, although that certainly is a game changer. I'm talking about creating support groups that become your new Family.

I meet a group of individuals monthly for a few hours. Not everyone can make it every time, but there are between five and eight of us in any given month

Some people might call them a mastermind group,' or' accountability partners, but to me, they're family."

Joanna was about to say something, but before she could, he continued, "Napoleon Hill spent 25 years interviewing the most successful people of his generation and wrote 'Think and Grow Rich' to distill the 17 lessons they shared.

Many people consider it one of the best personal development books ever written. I can't say I loved it, but I found three excellent chapters: passion, faith and the mastermind."

"You're well on your way Joanna. You're passionate, and your persistence shows me you have faith. Now it's time to work on the last part - you need a family to support you on your journey.

One of the pandemic's most significant effects on society was its isolationism.

Joanna had been confined to her apartment for the better part of an entire year.

She had avoided any social gatherings. She'd decided to go to that rooftop gathering a few months back because she wanted to drown her sorrows and didn't want to be alone.

"I realize," Anthony continued, "it's been tough for us the past year or so."

It was almost as if he could read her mind.

"Due to the situation, our group had to adapt. We decided to move online. Granted, it's not the same, but you do what you must."

Clubhouse was one of the beneficiaries of the pandemic and its ensuing lockdowns.

It was the breakthrough app of 2020, allowing people to jump into rooms to discuss any number of topics from venture capital, how to talk to investors, success habits of the wealthy, business books to meditation and even heavy metal.

Considering the circumstances, it was as close to a networking event as possible.

You knew who knew their stuff and who didn't. As it was audio based, your eyes weren't tricked by fancy clothes and nice cars.

Joanna hadn't spent much time on the app other than to check it out once or twice, but some of her friends raved about it.

With the lockdowns ending now and people emerging from their homes, people had started setting up meet-and-greets with people they had met through Clubhouse.

Digital going physical was becoming something of a trend.

Joanna remembered reading about how to differentiate the pro from the amateur in 'The Third Door' by Alex Banayan. One of the books on Anthony's list. Banayan's mentor had told him, "Using your phone makes you look like a chump. Always carry a pen in your pocket. The more digital the world gets, the more impressive it is to use a pen.

Anthony's phone buzzed again. That was his cue.

"We'll have to pick this up next time."

He picked up his gym back and headed to the locker room.

"Good luck with whatever it is you must do," Joanna replied.

Anthony looked over his shoulder and said, "Thanks."

Joanna sat down to finish off her workout.

Oprah Winfrey & Co.

Later that day, on her way home, Joanna was going over the day's lessons, and she thought about Oprah Winfrey.

Oprah had been born into poverty in rural Mississippi to a single teenage mother. Yet she rose to become one of the wealthiest and most influential people on the planet.

Her story is not unique, though.

J.K. Rowling was on welfare before writing the Harry Potter series that made her the world's first billionaire author.

Walt Disney was fired from a Missouri newspaper for "not being creative enough.

Stephen King was a troubled child and had multiple rejections before becoming "The Master of Horror."

Albert Einstein was told by one of his teachers he would never amount to anything.

Anita Roddick, the founder of the Body Shop, had a violent and alcoholic father.

Colonel Sanders lost his father by the age of five and lost four jobs before the age of seventeen. At the age of 73, he sold KFC for $2 million.

The odds were stacked against each of them, but as they say, the proof is in the pudding.

Many people like to blame their lives on the fault of their parents. That they weren't born to wealthy families, raised in a good neighborhood or that their parents had gotten divorced. While it's certainly true that such conditions put you behind the eight ball; as an adult, you must accept that you are in charge of your life.

You may not be able to choose where you start, but you have a say in where you end up.

That night Joanna came home, and while scrolling through her Twitter feed, she saw a picture that made her stop and think. Immediately, she grabbed a piece of paper and a pen and scribbled a few things down, including the picture which looked like this:

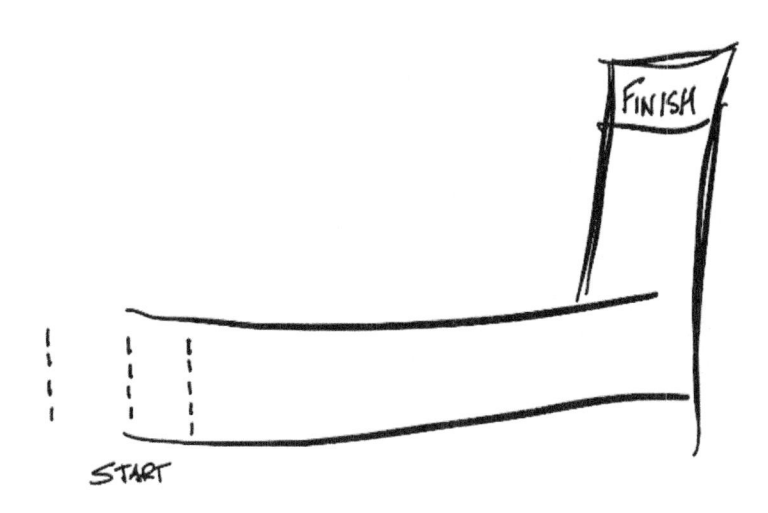

Most people start right on the starting line, but some people are lucky enough to be able to take a few steps forward. That's what family gives you: that little head start.

Unfortunately, some people start a few steps behind the starting line, perhaps because of an abusive father or a dysfunctional family.

Such things act as anchors, holding people from getting to the starting line. Home is not the only anchor; your school, city, and even your genes may hold you back.

But it's important to remember that regardless of where you start, the choices you make, the actions you take and how hard you work to determine where you end up in this race.

It's understandable when you're a child because children don't have control of their lives. They're dependent on the decisions of their parents and other people around them. People want to blame their family, relatives, siblings, circumstances, health, teachers and even the government for the predicaments they find themselves in.

However, as you grow, you get more control over your life. As an adult, where and how you live is up to you. How much money you save is up to you.

The jobs you take, the food you eat, the time you wake up, the amount you sleep, the games you play, the things you study, the books you read, the amount of TV you watch, the time you spend on social media, what you do on social media, they are all up to you.

You decide.

Not your parents.

You.

Joanna sat on the sofa, thinking about how fortunate she'd been to have such a supportive family. But now she was on a new journey and realized she'd need a new one.

CHAPTER 9

TAKING CONTROL OF YOUR SCHEDULE

Even though Joanna was becoming more comfortable with her schedule, she still needed to get better at managing some of the distractions so that they didn't consume her peace and her time.

The distractions were present in the background, but they didn't seem to derail her as much as before. However, it did happen occasionally.

When The Schedule Goes AWOL

When it did, she remembered what Anthony had said. 'Joanna, there'll be days when your schedule goes to the wall.

That's ok. Don't beat yourself up with the should've, could've and would've, narrative.'

"We're human, and it's ok for things not to go the way we want them to."

He said this would likely happen when we're tired, or an unexpected issue crops up.

In that instance, it's best to pause and take a moment before approaching your tasks.

He shared the Eisenhower Principle. Anthony suggested she look at her daily/weekly tasks and reorganize the list depending on urgency and importance.

The Eisenhower matrix is a simple and effective way to prioritize important and urgent tasks.

The matrix helps you to:

✓ Save time

✓ Be proactive in seeking solutions

✓ Focus on the right things

✓ Plan ahead

✓ Seek help when you need it

✓ Identify challenges upfront

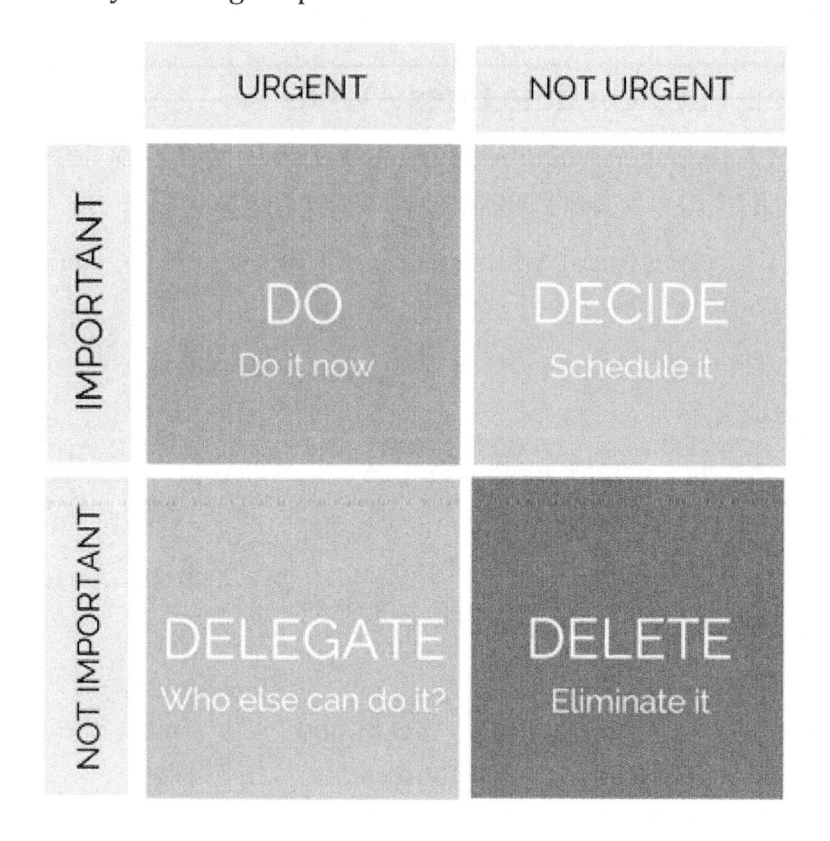

	URGENT	NOT URGENT
IMPORTANT	**DO** Do it now	**DECIDE** Schedule it
NOT IMPORTANT	**DELEGATE** Who else can do it?	**DELETE** Eliminate it

Anthony said, "look at what is important and urgent and try to focus on getting that done. The other less important tasks can be moved to a later time during the week".

He further explained that the mind is forgiving, but when you keep giving it the wrong 'fuel,' it tends to start working against you.

Words such as "I should" and "I would" start making the powerhouse feel suffocated, which leads to feeling anxious, stressed and worried.

Joanna thought about this for a moment. Once you're in this stressful state, it takes much longer to get back to normal. He suggested she look at the distraction from a different perspective.

Taking Back Control

Watch out for the words. If they are negative, they negatively impact the mind. Joanna came up with her analogy - junk food.

You look forward to eating a burger and fries, which boosts you, but a few hours later, you feel sluggish.

The same thing happens to the brain. If you give your engine the best fuel, it delivers superior results.

Joanna tried an exercise and watched her words for three hours one morning. She noticed a pattern and made a note of it in her journal.

"When I get a good night's sleep, I feel refreshed and can face my day with greater confidence.

If I have a late night or binge-watched Netflix, I wake up feeling a little tired, and then I start using negative words.

Yesterday was one of those days when I watched Netflix after having a productive day. I only planned to watch one show; three hours later, I was still up and went to bed late.

When I woke up, I felt tired and not my best self.

I first said to myself, "Oh no, I've got so much work to do, and I'm already behind schedule."

This meant that I started getting anxious about my tasks, and then I played the "I should have stopped watching Squid Game on Netflix at 10:45 pm instead of 12:30 am." I should have gone to bed earlier.

Joanna also noted that other distractions happened during the day, which could be a result of an unexpected phone call or email.

When that happened, she would apply the same rule of compassion and kindness towards herself.

Working From Home Loses Its Shine

It had initially been very challenging for Joanna, especially as it coincided with job hunting during the lockdown.

She felt she was dealing with two curveballs at the same time.

Like many, she eventually adjusted and got herself into a routine.

When she found her tempo, it helped her navigate the weeks and months ahead.

She knew the road ahead was very long, and it was doable with self-discipline for Joanna.

She missed the daily banter in the office, especially near the water cooler, as it helped her to let off steam or that's what she thought it did.

What she missed was having people around her.

It was easy to strike up conversations with colleagues in the office.

Outside of work, she had her old friends who were great listeners but were consumed with their own corporate or world dramas.

Anthony suggested she get a new 'family,' i.e. update her professional support circle.

Up until then, she muddled through with her blended social circle.

Build Your Support Group

Joanna wanted to connect with people who were experiencing similar challenges.

She realized it was very lonely working on her own, and having a couple of people to talk to, bounce ideas off each other or even learn together was essential.

Anthony was brilliant in helping her, but she didn't want to use him as her accountability partner.

So she was going to try and find different people.

At this stage, she didn't know where she would meet them, but as the saying goes, 'When the student is ready, the teacher will appear."

Clubhouse

Joanna finally joined Clubhouse, but she was still unsure.

She dropped into her first-ever session; the key guest was Elon Musk.

She remarked, "OMG, I can't believe I'm in the same room as him and listening to him live. I can even raise my hand and ask him a question."

She joined several rooms, including Entrepreneurs Mental Health, Why You Procrastinate, and Tech News Around The World.

In another session, she listened and was surprised by the quality of conversations in different rooms.

It felt like a live podcast with the audience as active participants.

People from all over the world connected, shared and exchanged information.

She felt at ease and put her hand up to speak.

Joanna was nervous but equally happy that she spoke in the 'Why You Procrastinate' Room.

She started following more experts and built her online presence.

She had worked on her Linkedin profile, hired and paid a web designer for $300 from Fiverr.com

Joanna was learning whilst listening, participating and sharing her views on Clubhouse.

Maybe this was why Anthony was keen for Joanna to try Clubhouse.

As Joanna quietly left the Clubhouse room, she opened her emails.

Joanna smiled when she received a message from an ex-colleague Sarah, who found working from home a bit of a struggle.

Working From Home Challenges

Joanna met Sarah at the Law firm, and she worked in the due diligence team. They worked on a couple of client projects together.

Sarah was younger, and Joanna would occasionally give her some work advice.

Joanna quickly emailed her back during her break because she knew what she was going through.

Hi Sarah,

It's great to hear from you, and I appreciate your reaching out. I went through WFH challenges not so long ago. Here are some top tips that you might find helpful.

- If tempted to spend the day in pajamas, don't. Get up as you would for work and dress in clothes that make you comfortable but presentable enough to jump onto a video call if needed. If you have client calls, decide on the appropriate dress code.

- Avoid checking mobiles every time you get a message. You probably wouldn't do it at work, so apply the same discipline.

- Minimize external distractions, ie taking calls from family & friends.

- I know you have young children at home. It's probably best to work out a suitable routine for you both. Tell the kids what's acceptable and what's not in terms of disturbing you.

- Deliver your best. Just because no one is watching doesn't mean it's ok to go on autopilot, no matter how tempting.

- Create a healthy boundary between work and non-work hours. This way, you have greater control in effectively planning your work and personal time.

- Look after yourself well. Take regular breaks and exercise where feasible. Working from home can be lonely. Develop a virtual support group with colleagues who are probably going through what you're going through.

- Keep in regular contact with your manager.

- Use your time to brush up on old skills and learn new ones.

Post-Pandemic, you might want to think about the following:

- What do you want? How many days work best for you?

- Where will you work at home? The kitchen table may not necessarily be the best long-term solution.

- Manage your expectations and that of others.
- Just because you're working from home doesn't mean you're always available and should respond to every email, notification or call immediately.
- Set boundaries because it's easy to blur work and personal boundaries and still burn the candle on both ends.
- Talk it over with your manager and see what would be ideal for you.
- Maybe have a trial period and then reassess again at a later date.
- Be flexible with your expectations.

Anyway, discipline doesn't mean you can't have fun. I've grown to love it over the last few weeks. Who knows if it may just spark great innovative ideas for you?

Warm regards,

Joanna

Creating Boundaries

Anthony had been mentoring Joanna for over a month, and she could see the benefits of having someone like him in her camp.

He was a grand champion of journaling and got her to capture her thoughts each evening. Today was no different.

Joanna was becoming more confident in setting her schedule and creating boundaries.

She spent 15 minutes capturing her thoughts in her journal in the evening. She wrote the following:

It's been a long day today, but a productive day. I'm tired tonight, so I'm not going to write a long post. Instead, I just wanted to capture the following:

- Did a time audit to find out where my time was going. I was surprised as to how much time I spent on small firefighting tasks.
- Creating Boundaries, especially when mom calls and friends message me.
- Find a dedicated space in the apartment and use this instead of moving around all over. The space near the window works best.
- Taking breaks helped me to get perspective and be focused.
- Keep the to-do list short each day.
- Boundaries get challenged when I try to do too much. The 'one last email' syndrome can mean spending more time than expected.
- I don't have to achieve everything all in one go
- Don't panic. Easier said than done, but keep calm because I need a level head to think next steps to make informed decisions

What I could do better tomorrow is:

- [ ] Work in time blocks instead of long stretches as its easy to do when WFH
- [ ] Instead of focusing on just one topic and trying to finish it spread out the topics over the week
- [ ] Use Friday afternoons to wrap up the week instead of letting it linger into the weekend
- [ ] Switching off at 6 pm and doing a fun activity

As Joanna became more comfortable with the significant change in her life, she picked up momentum with her short- and long-term plans.

Maybe she could use these notes to create a book for other washed-up ex-corporates one day. That would be another thing she could cross off her bucket list.

CHAPTER 10

A LEFT TURN

'Yes, finally', exclaimed Joanna.

After a long wait, she finally got a confirmation email with a contract from Harper and Co for some consulting work.

She'd also received a permanent job offer from Fisher Law firm earlier in the week.

Had the consulting work not come through, she would have been forced to take the Fisher Law deal.

Not because she wanted to but out of necessity. Bills don't just pay themselves.

Now she knew her efforts were finally paying off, and things were coming together, especially as she also had some freelance work with UpWork, which she enjoyed.

So, coupled with the contract, things were looking up, which put Joanna in high spirits for the rest of the morning.

She pondered for a moment and thought about her journey so far. Sometimes she wondered how she even got through those days straight after the redundancy.

Joanna let the uncertainty dictate her mood early on because she didn't know what to do. Then, she would wake up, go through the motions, and let things dictate her days.

In other words, she was at the mercy of her environment.

The first few weeks seem like a blur to her now.

Don't Take Your Foot Off the Accelerator

Joanna realized that she had taken her foot off the accelerator at the Law firm and gotten too comfortable.

She started to cruise in her career because she thought things were going well.

However, the alarm bells should have started ringing because complacency had led to stagnation.

Joanna also realized she'd been waiting for someone to recognize the superhuman effort she put in a week in and a week out.

Like many young professionals climbing the career ladder, Joanna had forgotten her dreams and goals. Instead, she focused on low-hanging career goals.

Joanna was naïve in thinking her firm would acknowledge the numerous sacrifices she made personally and professionally and reward her for her efforts.

But unfortunately, she never got to find out. Instead, she dealt with the aftermath of an unexpected seismic career shock.

If she were to make the journey again, she would spend more time developing herself and crafting her career.

She realized she had left this important work for her bosses to figure out.

Joanna knew her career was her responsibility.

However, she had to go through those days to get to the other side of the tunnel.

Light at the End of the Tunnel

When Joanna's job was made redundant, she shut herself away from others because she dreaded the how's-the-job-hunting-going question.

Joanna knew her family and friends meant well, but they weren't helping her by putting her on the spot.

The pandemic exacerbated the situation, and Joanna despaired from the lack of progress during the job hunt because it became a cumbersome grind.

She remembered throwing everything she knew at the job hunt, but her approach did not yield the desired results.

However, it was a blessing because she would never have discovered her strengths and learned to play them.

She also made peace with her departure from the law firm. As she grew over the last few months, she saw the career curveball for what it was - a business reality that had nothing to do with her as a person.

Life happens; the question is how you will deal with it.

Her self-awareness taught her that opportunities were endless for those willing to step forth. However, she would need to work hard consistently towards her goals.

Opportunities Aplenty

Joanna had reached out to her Alma Mater after receiving one of their digital newsletters.

Previously, the old Joanna would have deleted the email without reading it, but she clicked the link and opened it this time.

She read about the numerous achievements and awards her Alma Mater had received, but the careers section caught her eye.

She decided to reach out to them and see if she could speak to someone about offering her services as a guest speaker.

It turned out to be a good move because the Careers department was looking for new guest speakers, especially as the country opened up again.

Joanna put together a proposal for them regarding what topics she could discuss.

She thought it was a great 'win/win.

She readily agreed and could now add public speaking as part of her service offering.

Joanna was previously reluctant to speak at industry events, so she had come a long way.

Finally, however, she would talk in front of many students and alums who wanted to hear more about her law career and tips on getting into the industry.

Keep Learning

The months post the redundancy led her to meet some great people along the way.

She learnt many lessons from each one.

From Christina, she learnt to take care of her health. She invited Joanna to her Soul Cycle class, and Joanna felt good after her sessions.

Anthony taught her to trust her instincts and be unafraid to try new things.

Initially, she was overwhelmed by the work she needed to do, but she learned the power of goal-setting and prioritization.

As a result, she could chip away at her goals daily.

There were days when she didn't feel like it, and some were washouts, but she learnt to be kind to herself.

One thing she realized very quickly was avoiding the stop/start approach to learning. Procrastination was the biggest culprit.

Tomorrow seemed attractive only because it offered a false sense of hope.

Joanna learnt a painful truth very quickly: that stopping/starting goal setting was mentally exhausting. Plus, it killed any momentum she had.

Now she understood why many people failed to accomplish the BHAG (Big Hairy Audacious Goals), which she's read about in The Magic of Thinking Big by David J. Schwartz.

It had nothing to do with the lack of willpower; it was more to do with the lack of consistency.

Over time, she built momentum by doing a bit every day, not just when motivated to complete a task.

Joanna was diligent in creating her weekly schedule and adding a healthy time buffer each day to accommodate any unexpected disruptions.

Flexibility and adaptability were vital to success, along with hard and intelligent work.

Build Bridges

Whilst working for the law firm, Joanna limited her networking to people from the law industry.

However, she realized how limiting this approach was, and by doing so, she shut herself off from learning from non-law professionals.

She avoided networking events because she found them to be too transactional.

Now, Joanna learnt to engage in developing meaningful professional and personal relationships.

She also learned to build bridges without expectations.

Now, she enjoys building bridges with people from all walks of life. Joanna discovered the art of free learning simply by talking to others.

Joanna didn't automatically think, 'What's in it for me?' when she met new people?'

Instead, she appreciated each one for who they were by listening attentively.

Surprisingly, she also found that she had much to contribute, especially with the new projects she was working on.

In addition, other people were interested in her story.

Joanna found that many people she spoke to identified with her story, especially those still working in the corporate world.

They told her that things were okay for the time being, but they were losing their mojo fast.

The New World of Work

Boy, did Joanna know about losing her mojo?

Thankfully she rediscovered it again over the past few weeks and months, but it took a lot of effort, honesty and self-awareness.

The new normal was here to stay, and she quickly realized that what worked yesterday wasn't going to work today and tomorrow.

Joanna appreciated that she would need to engage in regular self and professional development.

It took Joanna a little while to understand her development needs initially, and she started using her journal to work it through.

When she looked back at her journal entries, she smiled when she read her earlier entries. They sounded so naïve, but that was a snapshot at the beginning of her growth.

Joanna found the SWOT (Strengths, Weakness, Opportunities and Threats) example very powerful. She spent 30 minutes each day for three days.

Her SWOT exercise helped her understand what was missing in her skills and experience repertoire.

Once she knew what was missing, she could start setting goals to help her achieve her objectives whilst simultaneously playing to her strengths to shift gears.

The Coffee Shop Revisited

She'd asked Anthony to meet her at her favorite coffee shop, the one she found herself in 4 months ago when she had just learned she'd been let go.

"Thanks for coming," Joanna said as Anthony walked over to where she was sitting.

Anthony sat down across from her and sunk into the comfortable chair.

"I can see why you like it here," he said as he looked around. It was modern but made to look antique-ish.

Pictures on the wall were from a mixture of famous and not-yet-famous NY photographers.

The chairs were oversized and looked like they belonged in a log cabin rather than in New York City.

Joanna told him the good news – her consulting gig and the offer to speak to her Alma Mater's MBA program.

Her efforts were not going unnoticed, but the most significant accomplishment had to be her shift in mindset.

Gone were the days of her outdated limiting beliefs, and Joanna spoke with a childlike enthusiasm.

Challenges no longer seem as a negative but as an opportunity for her to grow.

Her attitude alone was what had secured her the speaking gig.

She'd also rejoined Clubhouse and popped into a few different rooms.

Joanna told Anthony how she now had a weekly call with two people halfway across the world, one in England and the other in Japan.

She met them in a book club and found they shared her passion for growth.

Things were falling into place nicely though she hadn't found a full-time job that appealed to her.

Nonetheless, she could at least pay her bills, which was important.

She was confident she could do it.

She had the skill set, and she had the contacts. It wasn't a question of ability but one of resolve.

Did she want to take the risk or go back to the "safety" of corporate work?

It was a new day for Joanna, filled with excitement and adventure.

The one thing she knew was she didn't couldn't, no wouldn't, accept a job that didn't align with her passion.

Anthony's lessons had paid off physically, mentally and now financially.

One Last Piece of Advice

Anthony sat there for a good 10 minutes before saying anything.

He enjoyed listening to Joanna's story and just nodded or added the occasional "uh-huh."

In his youth, Anthony had dominated conversations, but the years had taught him the value of listening.

When Joanna finally stopped to take a sip of her coffee, she must have realized because she said, "Sorry for rattling on…I'm just so excited."

Anthony smiled and said, "May I give you one last piece of advice?"

Joanna leaned forward, eager to hear what he had to say.

"Please!"

"People work hard to be able to live a good life.

They work hard to buy a lovely house, get a nice car, go on nice trips with their family and take care of their kids.

And that's certainly a worthwhile goal. But not many people are truly happy at their jobs. It's more of a means to an end.

Most people work their entire lives at jobs they don't like to survive.

They hope that one day, through promotion, investments or pure luck, they'll be able to retire and enjoy their twilight years.

It's not the way to live.

You have to enjoy the journey as much as the destination. So, my advice to you is to ask yourself one important question when making any critical decisions.

"What's the question?" Joanna asked.

What Anthony said next surprised her. It was as simple as could be.

"Am I happy?"

He continued, "If you're happy doing what you're doing, then you can keep doing it.

Moreover, by applying the lessons I've shared with you, you'll do very well for yourself.

The question does come in many forms.

Do I like what I'm doing? Do I like the people I'm working with? And do I like the people I'm working for?

Let these questions guide you. Whether you go back to corporate life, work as a consultant or open your own business."

It was like he could read her mind.

The truth is being an entrepreneur is not for everyone. Some people flourish as entrepreneurs, and others flounder.

There are pros and cons to both. You need to find your niche."

Magazines like Entrepreneur or Forbes often explore how wonderful the life of an entrepreneur is.

People like Elon Musk, Richard Branson and Mark Cuban were treated like modern-day rockstars.

But people rarely hear about the hardships they endure to achieve their incredible success.

"Don't get me wrong," Anthony continued. "I love being an entrepreneur as I get to live life on my terms doing what I love.

I'm just saying it's not for everyone. But if you're happy, that's a good sign you're on the right path."

Joanna was happy. For the first time in a long time.

But despite her new work opportunities, she felt something was missing.

"Many people get stuck in one place, doing one job and never really seeing what else is there for them. Have you ever thought about moving to Austin?"

"Austin?"

"I have a friend working on a start-up and looking for a few good people. No promises. But if you like, I could pass along your name."

Joanna had to admit her love affair with the Big Apple had run its course.

The past few months had changed her. Her bank account prevented her from enjoying the NY nightlife, but the truth is told, she didn't miss it that much.

Moreover, New York was expensive and hadn't fully recovered from the damage caused by the lockdowns.

Austin might be good for her.

A fresh start.

The potential to join a company on the ground floor appealed to her.

Of course, everything could go wrong, but the past few months had taught Joanna how to deal with adversity.

Stay or go?

There were pros and cons both ways, but with Tesla headquarters being there, it was a city attracting a lot of attention.

Moreover, Texas had been able to handle the pandemic reasonably well, and the economy was strong.

It would be hard to say goodbye to the place she'd called home for ten years, but she knew better than to look a gift horse in the mouth.

"Ok, I'm in."

"After all, Anthony's friend could still say no," she thought.

"Great, I'll let him know."

A New Beginning

Joanna took one last look at her apartment, picked up her suitcases, and headed for the elevator.

She'd spent much of the past week packing boxes to prepare for the move.

She'd sent her boxes ahead to her new place, which her new boss had set up for her.

It had been two months since she'd said yes to the start-up job in Austin.

Joanna had to admit she had butterflies in her stomach, but they were the good kind that came with new adventures.

She'd had a farewell dinner the night before to say goodbye to her friends.

Most of her friends had been there, but Sam couldn't make it, so he insisted on driving her to the airport.

He was waiting downstairs for Joanna.

Appendix

Chapter 1 A Rough Day

Main Lesson: Things happen out of your control.

- Be prepared for a rainy day.
- Business is business. Don't take it personal.

Chapter 2 Health

Main Lesson: You can only be as productive as you feel.

- Food = fuel. Your diet determines a large portion of your health.
- Ironically, the more you exercise, the less sleep you need.
- Physiology precedes psychology. Exercise releases endorphins. Action creates feelings.

Chapter 3 Dealing with A Career Curveball

Main Lesson: Focus on What You Can Control.

- Don't try to control what's not for you to manage. If you do, you'll experience many conflicting emotions.
- When you face an uncertain situation or challenge, one of the things you can control is your attitude.
- Ask yourself the following question: What's the one thing I can control right now?
- A 'spray and pray' approach won't help you either. Why? It's a bit like trying to fire darts towards a dartboard in the dark.

- Take a breather. Sometimes trying to battle on is not productive. Imagine how frustrating it is trying to bang harder on a door that's not going to open. Instead, step back and take a breather. Why? It will help get perspective.

Chapter 4 Career Transformation

Main Lessons: Learn to Tune Out

- Don't worry about other people's judgments. Easier said than done, right? You have more power than you think.
- Ask yourself 'Whose voice am I tuning into right now?
- I am making the most of each day. Think of each day as a blank canvas that provides an opportunity to create the day as you wish.
- Start the day as you mean to go on. When you start the day with the right intention, you won't be swayed too much by the day's events.
- A Career SWOT helps you focus. How? You'll enhance your self-awareness and start exploring different opportunities to see what's possible and what's not.

Chapter 5 Adjusting to the New Normal

Main Lesson: Change can lead to growth and development

- Create your routine. If you complete the smallest of tasks each day, it will give you a sense of control.

- Find your anchors. These could be anything including family, friends, places, objects, hobbies or experiences or anything which gives you a sense of anchoring.

- Be unafraid to experiment with different things. It's easy to keep doing what you have always done, but varying your tasks will help you find new insights or ideas.

- Unlearn to relearn. What worked yesterday might not be tomorrow, and for your skills to remain competitive, it's essential to learn, unlearn and relearn without judgment.

- Keep a journal. A journal is a great way to capture your journey. Spending 10 minutes each day helps to shape your ideas, growth and creativity.

Chapter 6 Productivity

Main Lesson: Focus on the little things that make the biggest difference.

- Health is where it all starts. "You can only be as productive as you feel."

- Habits determine 40% of your success/failure. Negative habits are default, so we must actively create positive ones.

- Personal Development
    - Jim Rohn (Mindset)
    - Zig Ziglar (Mindset)
    - Napoleon Hill (Mindset)
    - Tony Robbins (High Performance)

- Brendon Burchard (High Performance)
- Strategies
    - Use the 80/20 rule to its fullest.
    - Add more strategies to increase productivity.
- Technology acts as an amplifier. Use tech to simplify / enhance / speed up your business and private life.

Chapter 7 Creating the right environment

Main Lesson: Maximize Hybrid Work

- As many people adapt to the new world of work, it's essential to create a working environment that works best for you. Be honest and ask yourself how you would like to work.
- Share your thoughts with your manager, who will help you find a win/win solution.
- I am eliminating the distractions. Watch out for the time and energy zappers. Identify and make a note of five of them.
- If you're working from home, create a boundary between work/home. You may wish to consider where you work, what time you finish and how you manage the notifications on your phone/laptop.
- Keep the to-do lists short. The more tasks you have on the list, there is a danger of feeling overwhelmed, especially if they haven't been checked off.

Chapter 8 The Mastermind

Main Lesson: You are the average of the five people you spend the most time with.

- Virtual Mentors
  - Dan Kennedy (Marketing)
  - Robert Cialdini (Influence)
  - Stephen Covey (Business)
  - John Maxwell (Leadership)
  - Robert Kiyosaki (Investment)
- Monthly meetings
  - Variety is the spice of life (learn from people with fresh eyes).
  - 5-10 people (one or two might be absent).
  - Take turns talking without interruption (Clubhouse style).
- Reflect values
  - Find people that share similar goals.
- Language reflects beliefs
  - Words have power.

Chapter 9 Taking Control of Your Schedule

Main Lesson: Make your schedule work for you

- Do you control your schedule, or does it hold you?

- Build your support network. Reaching out for help when you need it, not only when it's just become critical.

- Take regular breaks. It may seem obvious, but taking regular intervals means recharging your mind and body regularly.

- Watch out for the 'one more quick email/phone call ' mindset. Why? It might take longer than you anticipated.

- Have a little buffer in your schedule for unexpected demands on your time. If your plan is tightly packed, you may struggle to accommodate any last-minute interruptions.

Chapter 10 Left Turn

Main Lesson: Be open to new opportunities.

- Keep learning to be able to take advantage of new opportunities.

- Networking is key as the more people you get to know, the more opportunities you will become aware of.

- Try to align yourself with companies and individuals you feel share your views and goals.

- Being happy will allow you to work longer and harder than if you're not. Find ways to be happy.

Additional Information

We put together a Job-Hunter's Daily Checklist for you.

- Have a little buffer in your schedule for unexpected demands on your time. If your plan is tightly packed, you may struggle to accommodate any last-minute interruptions.
- Don't check the mobile phone the first thing upon waking up. Doing so interrupts the mindset needed to focus.
- Eat timely meals to have ample energy to get through the day.
- Clear the working space of any clutter.
- Research the day before so the day can start dealing with the job hunt instead of mundane administrative tasks.
- Keep the To-do list to a minimum.
- Set achievable tasks daily and cross this list off upon completing the task.
- Work in blocks of time. Anything between 25 minutes to 45 minutes, and don't forget to take a break.
- Take breaks regularly as this prevents burnout.
- Do the complex tasks first.
- Use a spreadsheet or note app to make a list of companies and fill the sheet in as the job hunt progresses.
- Evaluate the day and make necessary changes to improve moving forward.

- Celebrate the small wins.
- Set times to check your phone/ social media.
- Working smarter is better than working long hours for no real reason.
- Get support. Building a support network, especially when working alone, is essential as the job hunt can be physically draining.

Printed in Great Britain
by Amazon